Socialnomics

Ashley

BEN—

All the
BEST!

Erik Qualman

Socialnomics

How Social Media Transforms
the Way We Live and Do Business

Erik Qualman

WILEY

John Wiley & Sons, Inc.

Published by John Wiley & Sons, Inc., Hoboken, New Jersey.

Published simultaneously in Canada.

For general information on our other products and services or for technical support, please contact our Customer Care Department within the United States at (800) 762-2974, outside the United States at (317) 572-3993 or fax (317) 572-4002.

Wiley also publishes its books in a variety of electronic formats. Some content that appears in print may not be available in electronic books. For more information about Wiley products, visit our web site at www.wiley.com.

Library of Congress Cataloging-in-Publication Data:

Qualman, Erik, 1972–
  Socialnomics : what happens in Vegas stays on YouTube / how social media transforms the way we live and do business / by Erik Qualman.
      p. cm.
  Includes index.
  ISBN 978-0-470-47723-6 (cloth)
  1. Internet marketing. 2. Social media. 3. Social networking. 4. Electronic commerce. I. Title.
  HF5415.1265Q83 2009
  330.9—dc22

2009008841

Printed in the United States of America.

9 8 7 6 5 4 3 2 1

Contents

- Why is there a need for social media? Why has it become the most popular activity on the Web in a span shorter than three years?
- Despite fragmentation caused by the Web, people still desire an understanding of what the majority of people are doing. Social media is that mechanism.
- In the future, we will no longer look for the news; rather, the news will find us, or we will create it. That future is now.

- Two distinct forms of behavior have emerged in the social media age. The first one is preventative; for example, you may hide alcoholic drinks during photos, or you may avoid that "harmless" photo with the two attractive lifeguards on your next business trip.
- Similar constructs apply to corporations. Companies are thinking hard about actions that could cause a negative reaction within the blogosphere or social graph.
- While preventative behavior is somewhat of a drag compared to the socially unaccountable freedom our parents enjoyed in the 1960s, it's a good thing on the whole. It's making us adhere to the old adage "live your life as if your mother is watching."

- The second, more exciting change is braggadocian behavior. As people continue to microblog and update their status on social networks, it soon becomes a competition of who's doing the coolest thing. What once took place only occasionally around the watercooler is now happening in real time.
- As a society, this is a good thing. It allows people to take stock of their collective lives and what they're doing throughout the day, rather than letting years go by and looking back on a wasted youth, saying "what did I do with my life?"

- Is it any wonder that the television viewing audience is shrinking by the minute? People are actually living their own lives rather than watching others. As a company, it's imperative that you produce products and services so that people not only want to be associated with your brand, but also take ownership of it.

Social Media Is In
Out: Reality TV
In: Reality social media

- For an indication of how powerful social media is, we need look no further than Barack Obama's meteoric rise to power.

- Socialommerce: Billions of dollars will be made in and around social media; a majority from search queries around products and services. Consumers will have the ability to see what their friends and colleagues found relevant, researched, purchased, and commented on. We've always valued word of mouth, social media puts it on steroids by allowing you to search for it.
- Social media eliminates multiple individual redundancies in society. This is a tremendous benefit in saving people's time, energy, and frustration.
- It is mission critical for companies to understand that the impact of social media shifts traditional business practices across marketing,recruiting,manufacturing, etc.

- People play various roles in their own lives and take on different personalities depending on where they are or with whom they are interacting. People have their work personas that are much different from their nightlife personas, which in turn are different from their family personas, and so on.
- The same holds true for corporations; on one hand, a company donates millions to save-the-planet-type funds, but on the other hand, they dump millions of gallons of toxic waste into the clean water supply.
- The transparency and speed of information flow caused by social media mitigates this type of social schizophrenic behavior. What does this mean for companies and individuals?

Acknowledgments

Socialnomics could not have been completed without the help of many friends and family. First and foremost, my beautiful wife Ana Maria served a dual role of sounding board and support coach. My immediate family of Dad, Mom, Jay, Helene, Matt, Mary Alison, and my loving grandparents made certain to tell me when things weren't up to standard, but in a nice way. Encouragement came from my newest family members, the Lozanos: Margarita, Fernando, Jose, and Stephanie. A special thanks goes out to my talented editors, Shannon Vargo, Linda Indig, and Beth Zipko, for having both the skill and patience to make this happen. To talented authors Tim Ash and Brian Reich for introducing me to John Wiley & Sons—a truly class outfit. And finally, to numerous friends and family who kept giving me positive reinforcement and ideas, just when they were needed most—you know who you are and it meant more than you know.

About This Book

This book does not need to be read from start to finish like a sultry novel, nor should it be. Rather, it provides useful insight into changes in macrotrends, behaviors, and constructs as a result of social media. Just like social media itself, this book is written in sporadically digestible sound bites, and by the magic of my wonderful editor Shannon Vargo, is arranged so that you, the reader, can easily select an example, particular principle, or case study that is relevant to you or your company. So, while this work will not win any *Grammar Girl* awards, I hope you find it informative, educational, and entertaining.

Updates and augmentations to this book can be found at www.socialnomics.net.

I love hearing from my readers at twitter@equalman or equalman@gmail.com—feel free to disagree or shower me with affection. I adhere to my promise of personally responding..

Introduction

It's a People-Driven Economy, Stupid

In 1992, James Carville coined the phrase "It's the economy, stupid."[1] This simple phrase was a major driver behind why Bill Clinton became our forty-second president. Much has happened since 1992, with the most powerful change being the ubiquitous adoption and assimilation of the Internet. The Internet has revolutionized almost every facet of our business and personal lives. This last statement about the Internet is hopefully not news to anyone reading this book.

What is news however is that, today, we are in the early stages of yet another far-reaching revolution. This revolution is being driven by people and enabled by social media. That is why almost two decades later we are taking liberty with Carville's famous quote by adjusting it to: "It's a *people-driven* economy, stupid." Although only a slight modification of words, it's a drastic adjustment in philosophy and in how people and businesses are changing and will continue to evolve in the coming years. Barack Obama understood that it was now a people-driven economy, and he rode this philosophy and strategy all the way to the White House. He was able to leverage social media to mobilize the young and old alike, to go from an unknown senator in 2004 to the most powerful man in the world four short years later. In his historic victory speech, he acknowledges this:

I will never forget who this victory truly belongs to. It belongs to you.... We didn't start with much money or many endorsements. Our campaign was not hatched in the halls of Washington.... It was built by working men and women who dug into what little savings they had to give $5, $10, and $20 to the cause.[2]

Socialnomics is a massive socioeconomic shift. Yet, some of the core marketing and business principals of the last few centuries will still apply; whilst other basic principals will become as extinct as the companies that continue to try to force them on the unwilling public.

We are already seeing the economic potential of social media in its ability to reduce inefficient marketing and middlemen. Million-dollar television advertisements are no longer the king influencer of purchase intent. People referring products and services via social media tools is the new king. It is the world's largest referral program in history. There is also less need to subscribe to costly newspapers when consumers are pushed more relevant and timely free content from their peers via social media. The news finds us. All of this can be done easily from the comfort of home or while on the go with mobile devices. These paradigms and shifts, along with many others, are discussed in the forthcoming pages. The end result is that everything from purchasing a baby carriage to drafting a last will and testament is easier and cheaper for the consumer and more profitable for the seller.

Social media also eliminates millions of people performing the same tasks (multiple individual redundancy) over and over. If a new father sees via social media that 14 of his closest friends have purchased the same brand and model baby seat and they all express glowing reviews, he will not waste hours on research, as it has already been done by people he trusts. This recaptures billions of hours that can be redistributed toward the betterment of society. Today's winners are not the result of Madison Avenue, Blueblood Political Parties, or Monopolistic Distributors. As a result of the ease and speed with which information can be distributed amongst the social graph, the winners today are great products and services—which ultimately means that people win. Companies can elect to do business as usual at their own peril. We are at the start of a newer and brighter world for consumers and businesses; this is the world of socialnomics.

Chapter One

Word of Mouth Goes World of Mouth

Why is there even a need for social media? In less than three years, it became the most popular activity on the Web,[1] supplanting pornography for the first time in Internet history. Even search engines weren't powerful enough to do that.

Remember several years back when the last three to four seconds of many television commercials prompted viewers to use various AOL keywords? You don't see or hear that anymore do you? What do you see? People are sending this traffic to social networks. A very prominent example of this is CBS, which sends a majority of its March Madness basketball traffic, not to its own web site, but to www.facebook.com/brackets.

Why has social media's popularity been so meteoric? This rapid ascent is due in large part to its ability to help people avoid *information indigestion*. At first glance, this would seem counterintuitive because social media, in its inherent nature via status updates, microblogs, social bookmarks, video sharing, photo commenting, and so on, actually produces more content and information. Because of this increase in information, you would think that it would cause more confusion, not less. But, when we dive deeper, we can see why this is not the case.

In his groundbreaking book, *The Long Tail,* Chris Anderson eloquently describes the ability of the Internet within free markets to easily and effectively service small interest groups:

The great thing about broadcast is that it can bring one

show to millions of people with unmatchable efficiency. But it can't do the opposite—bring a million shows to one person each. Yet that is exactly what the Internet does so well. The economics of broadcast era required hit shows—big buckets—to catch huge audiences. Serving the same stream to millions of people at the same time is hugely expensive and wasteful for a distribution network optimized for point-to-point communications. Increasingly, the mass market is turning into a mass of niches.[2]

As we have seen, this is very powerful stuff. *The Long Tail* is great for individualism, however at the same time, it greatly fragments the market. Life was much simpler when we knew that all our world news would come from *Time* and *Life* magazines. Fragmentation can be a stress-inducing issue for people.

As human beings, we have the dichotomous psychological need to be our own individual, yet we also want to feel that we belong to and are accepted by a much larger social set. People are willing to keep *open running diaries* as a way to stay connected because their ultimate desire is to feel accepted.

The younger the generation, the less concerned they are about privacy.

> If you can make something more relevant to me by having less privacy, well that is a small price to pay.
> —Bill Tancer, General Manager, Global Research, Hitwise

Part of this lies in a yearning to have a clear understanding of what the majority of people are doing.

It was much easier to know what the majority was doing when all you had to do was tune into Casey Kasem's *American Top 40* to find out the latest and greatest in music or to flip through *Vogue* magazine to quickly grasp every fashion trend.

Who Cares What You Are Doing?

Why do I care if my friend is having the most amazing peanut-butter-and-jelly sandwich? Or that someone is at her kid's dance recital? These types of questions are often posed by someone who doesn't understand social media rather than by someone who hasn't embraced social media; there is a difference. These questions are usually posed by someone who is frustrated because they don't understand what social media is about.

Heavy social media users actually don't care about every little thing happening in their friend's lives all the time. Yes, there are the exceptional few who view every little post, photo, or comment. Individual users make personal choices about how they establish their settings and, more important, viewing behavior.

This is similar to a BlackBerry or iPhone where users can customize their settings so that the unit vibrates every time a message comes in or they can disable that setting and download messages on their time, thereby avoiding *crackberry* syndrome (addictive immediate response to every incoming message).

The key with social media is that it allows you to easily stay abreast of people you want to stay connected with via casual observation. Someone might argue, "well I already don't have enough time in my day, how can I possibly follow anybody else or keep those following me informed? I can't waste my time like that!" This is a fundamental misunderstanding! One of the key maxims of this book is that *wasting time on Facebook and social media actually makes you more productive.* Let's look at an example with a fictitious character dubbed Sally Supermarket.

We find Sally Supermarket at her favorite place and namesake. It's Fourth of July weekend, so a few of the checkout lanes are much longer than normal. It's going to be roughly a 10-minute wait until she reaches the cashier. During these 10 minutes she can:

A. Flip through a magazine she has no interest in.
B. Be rude and place a call on her cell phone. Most likely annoying the others in line around her and potentially the person receiving the call as well, because it's loud in the supermar-

ket, and she might have to hang up the call at any time.

C. Check on updates from her social media.

D. Ruminate about how upset she is that she has to wait in line for 10 minutes, which she definitely doesn't have time for.

Sally chooses option C, and here's what occurs:

- *Sally's status:* "Bummed that the supermarket is out of mayonnaise—I was planning to make my cold chicken curry salad for the annual picnic tomorrow."
- *Friend 1's status:* "Excited to be boarding a plane to DC for the weekend!"
- *Friend 2's status:* "Who knew my kids would love mandarin oranges in a can?"
- *Friend 3's status:* "I'm pregnant!"
- *Sally's daughter's status:* "Excited! Got an A on my psychology exam—off to get a Frappuccino to celebrate!"
- *Friend 4's comment:* "Sally, plain yogurt is a great substitute for mayo—use a third more curry than normal to kill the bitterness. I recommend Dannon. It's healthy too!"
- *Friend 3's status:* "Going in for first ultrasound. We've decided not to find out if the baby is a boy or a girl ahead of time."
- *Friend 5's post:* "Great video on bike decorating for the Fourth of July is found here: www.tinyurl.com/4th/."

After reading the status updates from her friends on her phone, Sally still has about four minutes before she'll be at the front of the checkout lane, so she runs to get some plain yogurt (like her friend recommended). While checking out she sees a $10 gift card for Starbucks hanging above the magazines, which she purchases with the intent of mailing it to her daughter as a surprise congratulations for doing well on her exam and to let her know she's thinking about her.

Sally will see Friend 3 tomorrow at the picnic and be able to congratulate her on her pregnancy. Staying up to date on Friend 3 means that Sally won't spend time speculating whether Friend 3 was just putting on extra weight. Sally can also avoid asking if the couple knows whether the baby will be a boy or girl because Sally already knows that they are waiting based on Friend 3's last updated social media message. Sally knows from firsthand pregnancy experience how tiring answering the "Do you know if it's a boy or girl?" question can become—if only she had social media back then!

On the way home, Sally's husband calls her.

"Hey, honey, I'm on my way home from the supermarket—how are you?"

"Struggling—Jack and I are trying to decorate his bike, but it's not looking so hot, and the crepe paper keeps tearing in the spokes."

"Not sure if this will help, but Friend 5 just bookmarked a video about bike decorating—maybe you could check it out for some ideas."

This Sally Supermarket example is a little played up for the purpose of illustration, but it certainly isn't far-fetched. This is a simple example of why social media isn't just for teenagers with too much idle time on their hands.

Foreign Friends Are Not Forgotten

This depiction by German-based social media user, Christoph Marcour, is a quick example of how social media can easily keep us globally connected:

> One thing I enjoy the most about social media is staying in touch with my friends in America. Before, I would occasionally travel to the United States for work; primarily to New York and Houston. I was generally very busy leading up to these trips and often didn't have time to e-mail or call my friends—all of which lived in Indianapolis. My friends from Indy also traveled for work quite a bit. So, ironically, we'd often be in the same city at the same time and not know it till months later.
>
> That doesn't happen anymore, now we have the chance to see each other once or twice a year. Because even if I'm not directly reaching out to them if I put in my status "packing for New York" or "Bummed that my flight to Houston is delayed," they see that, just as I see similar items that they are updating.[3]

Search Engines and Social Media

The Internet's greatest strength—rapid and cheap sharing of information—is also its greatest weakness. Search engines have and will continue to help users quickly access the one morsel of information they need out of the trillions of bytes of data. The inherent fault of search engines is that the user needs to know what they are looking for in the first place. For example, if users type in "Great Father's Day Gift" they do receive some helpful nuggets, but the results are often an overwhelming sea of confusion. And, if what you need is not on the first results page, it might as well not be anywhere because only roughly 5 percent of users go to the second page.

With the excess of information on the Web, people require a tool to make sense of it all, social media is that mechanism.

Search engines are getting better and better in understanding our individual search needs. Search engines have advanced technologically to recognize that when my 13-year-old cousin searches for "Paris Hilton" she is looking for the pseudocelebrity, but that when my mother searches for "Paris Hilton," she wants a hotel room in the City of Lights.

While these are nice improvements, if the searcher types in generic terms like "chocolate" or "shoes" the results will be relatively the same as everyone else's results. So, even though search results are getting better, you still can't type in "best rib-eye steak in New York" and quickly get what you are looking for. The advancement in semantic search will largely depend on who wins the search engine wars. If a virtual monopoly exists (e.g., Google), the advancement in search technology could potentially be slow. Someone could argue that the core offering and search engine results have not advanced much in the past five years. This isn't surprising given Google's relative dominance of the space over that time. Can one blame Google for not changing things too radically? Why would they try to *fix* something that is making record profits for their shareholders? This isn't a book about search, but we touch on it because social media and search are so closely tied to each other.

In fact, search engines are, rightfully so, viewing social media sites as competition—people are already going to wikipedia.org directly if they are on a fact-finding mission and starting to search within MySpace and Facebook for celebrities and other people. For the best articles on a subject, they may search Digg, Delicious, or another social bookmarking site. As we discuss in Chapter Five "Socialommerce," consumers will soon search Facebook, hi5, Orkut, and so on for products and services they want to research and/or purchase. So, Google's strongest competition may not be other search engines (Yahoo, MSN, Ask, etc.), but social media, instead.

Google and other search engines are recognizing this shift, and they are trying to make their offerings more social. In January 2009, Google introduced Google SearchWiki, giving users the ability to hit buttons that either promote a search (place it higher in that individual user's rankings) or demote a search result. This is a good advancement. Previously if a user disagreed with the search results, there was nothing they could do about it. The most exciting feature, one that gives further credibility to what we discuss throughout this book, is that Google introduced the ability for users to post comments about specific search results. All searchers can see these comments. Google's success in the social media space (e.g., SearchWiki) will be dependent on user uptake (just like *Wikipedia* wouldn't be successful if only 200 people contributed). Old and new players alike are racing to win the battle of social search.

We No Longer Search for the News—It Finds Us

We no longer search for the news; rather, the news finds us. This is evident when looking at key newspaper statistics. According to third quarter 2008 data from the Newspaper Association of America, advertising revenue for newspapers declined 18.1 percent, national advertising sales fell 18.4 percent, classifieds sank 30.9 percent, and online advertising sales dropped 3 percent.[4]

During the 2008 U.S. presidential election, one of *Saturday Night Live*'s (*SNL*) cast members, Tina Fey, was a dead ringer for Republican vice presidential nominee Sarah Palin. There were several skits done by Fey mimicking the vice presidential hopeful, and some argue that it played a large role in the election itself. The most popular of these episodes was the premier. What was interesting about this five-minute video was (1) the popularity of it and (2) where people watched the video clip.

NBC estimated that over 50 million viewed the "Palin Skits." According to research conducted by Solutions Research Group, more than half of the people who saw this *SNL* video viewed the clips over the Internet.[5] Many viewed it on the popular social video network YouTube; while the majority of others had it pushed to them and played right within their social media network, whether that was Facebook, MySpace, hi5, or something else.

As a result, *SNL*'s television viewership increased more than 50 percent over the previous year (2007), allowing NBC to profit from both ends of the spectrum (online exposure and TV ratings). The power of Socialnomics isn't just online; it can also drive activity in the opposite direction—to the offline world. This makes sense because the roots of social media and the social graph come from an offline world (book clubs, men's clubs, garden clubs, athletic clubs). It is just that technology has enabled us to go to a whole new level with our networks.

Old marketers used to conjure up 30-second commercials that were so entertaining that they would be discussed around the watercooler. However, what happens when the watercooler now exists for the sole purpose of dispensing water? Watercooler conversations are now happening online in real time.

There's no longer a need to wait until Monday morning to catch up because the speed of social media already has us all well informed. By seeing a few updates from various social media tools or from an aggregator, your friends probably have a good idea about where you were, how the weather was where you were, if you had any travel complications, whether you got a new puppy, whether you watched or attended a major event, whether you liked it, whether you had a fun weekend, and so on.

Newspapers and Magazines Diminish in Power

People will still catch up around the watercooler, but the conversation will be a little more detailed and specific rather than the traditional small talk. This on a whole is a good thing because it helps you learn more about people by getting more information all the time. You don't need to ask them how the weather was on their trip or what their new puppy looks like because you probably have seen their updates, photos, or videos. Instead, you can ask about the characteristics and personality of the puppy, and so on. This allows for the establishment of a quicker and more profound connection between individuals. If we are no longer walking down to the end of our driveways in anticipation of reading what is going on in the world, if we are no longer even going onto our favorite Internet news sites to find the news, what does it mean for various news outlets and the businesses that support them?

We have shifted from a world where the information and news was held by a few and distributed to millions, to a world were the information is held by millions and distributed to a few (niche markets). This has huge ramifications for traditional newspapers. The Internet caused major newspapers and magazines to rethink their business models. While these traditional mediums were still trying to grasp how to handle the upshot of blogs and user-generated content, social media suddenly came along, causing yet another significant upheaval in the status quo. In 2008, it was estimated that traditional newspapers would see a drop of 23.4 percent in revenues.[6] And 2009 can almost be labeled as the year the traditional newspaper died. *PC Magazine* is a good example of a periodical that experienced this macroshift first-hand. Launched in 1982, *PC Magazine* was such an icon in the tech world that at one point advertisers lined up in droves. (Sometimes causing certain issues to exceed 600 pages!)

PC Magazine closed the doors on their print version in November of 2008, moved all of their operations online, and renamed their online publication *PC Mag*. The move was necessary, even though they were in a relatively good position with revenue still in the tens of millions of dollars and digital already accounting for 70 percent of the *PC Mag* brand's revenues. Their online revenues have grown an average of 42 percent since 2001. *PC Mag* brand's revenues grew 18 percent in Q3, 2008.[7]

Traditional newspapers and magazines need to recognize that people are having their news pushed to them from friends and automated free subscriptions. This means newspapers and magazines need to change what their content delivers—otherwise the decline will continue. Newspapers should no longer be reporting the news; instead, they should be commenting on the news and what it means.

This book is actually a microcosm of this phenomenon. By the time this goes to print, many of the news items in this book will be outdated; in fact, some web sites listed in this book will no longer be market leaders or even exist at all. There may only be a handful of paper newspapers left as well. Hence, the importance for the material in this book, as well as in newspapers and magazines is to provide helpful commentary on what the news means and be able to identify constructs that have occurred before and will potentially occur again.

This continues to present an uphill battle for magazines and newspapers because they will need to have the best and brightest columnists and experts. But how do they retain these experts when their platform is no longer as strong as it once was? In the past, newspapers had almost full control because they managed the distribution. Today, the experts (i.e., writers, journalists, reporters, bloggers) have increased leverage because the price to entry for them to gain mass distribution is close to zero. While it still means something to have the *Wall Street Journal* on your résumé, it doesn't mean nearly as much as it once did.

Playboy and the *Sports Illustrated* Swimsuit Issue Are Stripped Down

A salient example of this is the once famed *Sports Illustrated* Swimsuit Issue. People in the 1980s and 1990s used to talk in anticipation for weeks prior to the Swimsuit Issue landing in mailboxes across the country. The most popular person in school or the office that week was whoever received the magazine and brought it in. *Sports Illustrated* was able to charge up to three times its usual rates to advertisers.

As a supermodel, landing on the cover of this issue was life changing. That was then, this is now. The luster of this issue quickly faded with the advent of the always available photograph and video on the Internet. When's the last time you heard the *Sports Illustrated* Swimsuit Issue in a conversation? It went from part of pop culture to irrelevance. Even Hugh Hefner's venerable *Playboy* in 2009 reduced its guaranteed magazine subscriber base 13 percent, from 3 million to 2.6 million. Christie Hefner, daughter of the founder, stepped down as CEO at the start of 2009.[8]

Craigslist, LinkedIn, Monster, CareerBuilder, Simply Hired and many others have eviscerated the one-time newspaper monopoly in recruitment advertising since the technology bubble burst, resulting in a loss of $4.9 billion, or 56.3 percent, of classified revenues between 2000 and 2007.[9]

The first step that some major periodicals took was to place their content online; this was a logical step. Of course they still needed to make money, and the model that they understood was subscription based. This worked well for a few years for major publications like the *New York Times* and *Wall Street Journal;* but if you have a good understanding of Socialnomics, you can see how over the long haul this is a somewhat flawed strategy. To effectively leverage the social graph, every company needs to understand that they need to make their information easily transferable.

Idaho Bloggers Are Better than New York Reporters

It's important to free your content from being trapped in a "walled garden" because people have quickly grown accustomed to the news finding them, and there is no turning back. That is a key construct of the book, the world as it was, no longer is. So good, bad, or indifferent, it is a fact that will not change.

People expect and demand easy access to their news; any hurdle, no matter how small, can kill potential distribution, eventual effectiveness, and ultimate viability. So let's quickly showcase an A-B comparison of how this works in Socialnomics.

News Site A

Site A is one of the world's largest and most well known newspapers. Historically they have generated revenue from print advertising, as well as paid subscriptions. In the past decade, they have put even more information on their web site, along with additional video content, multimedia, and so on. They have seen tremendous growth in their online revenue, but it's not enough to offset the loss incurred by their traditional offline revenue model. They still have a large staff of expensive expert writers, large office buildings that need to be maintained, along with trucks and various overhead to distribute the paper. As a result of these large costs, they require a paid subscription and login for their online content in the hopes of generating enough revenue to offset these costs.

Blog Site B

Jane the Blogger works out of her house in Boise, Idaho. She has plenty of time to write because she works only three days a week in the state courthouse. She uses a popular free blogging tool (e.g., Word Press, TypePad, Blogger) and pays $20 per year to have the vanity URL www.idaho-senators.com. She likes to stay current with events outside of Idaho and pays for a subscription to News site A. Her husband is a big Boise State football fan and gets a free subscription to the *Idaho Statesman,* and Jane enjoys reading the political section. Her only other cost is the time she spends reading the political section. One could argue that in this instance this is no cost at all because she finds intrinsic value (aka enjoys) in discussing the political topics on her blog about Idaho's senators.

To keep abreast of the latest news on her two senators, she uses free social media tools and alerts to push the news her way when either of the two senator's names is mentioned. She also carves out time to review and edit the various wikis (e.g., *Wikipedia*) across the Web on each respective senator. Her interest started when her friend, Julie Patterson from high school was elected to the senate seat. Patterson still holds her senate seat in Idaho.

Situation

The other Idaho senator (i.e., not Patterson) is involved in a drunk driving accident early one Saturday morning where he is at fault. There was one other passenger in the car, the senator's babysitter, and she was killed in the accident. The driver of the other car is a Supreme Court judge who was in Idaho on vacation. The Supreme Court judge is in critical condition at a local Boise hospital.

Jane the Blogger finds out about the accident from one of her friends from the courthouse prior to it appearing on local or national news. She is already intimately familiar with the Idaho senator, so no background is required; in fact, she knows that he has a history of overindulging with booze and has had a previous DUI incident that went through her courthouse a few years before he became a senator.

Meanwhile, News Site A's field reporter for that area is on vacation, and so they assign it to a reporter who sits in their Manhattan headquarters. This reporter is not at all familiar with the Idaho senator and immediately goes to her favorite search engine and types in the senator's name. Guess whose site comes up in the top five rankings on the search engine? You guessed it www.idaho-senators.com. The reporter reads background information on the senator and then hops on a flight to Boise. While on the flight, she begins writing the story. Jane the Blogger and the reporter both post stories about the event. Because of her background and experience on the subject matter, Jane the Blogger posts her story an hour or two before News Site A. Not only that, to pre-sell her more in-depth story, she originally breaks the news she received from the courthouse via a micro-blogging tool like Twitter. She immediately becomes the recognized expert on this story. Micro-blog posts were the first to break such noteworthy news events as the 2009 US Airways water crash landing in New York and the 2008 California forest fires, and will play an important role moving forward.

The purpose of this example isn't to showcase what produces better stories—blogs or traditional reporters—there are plenty of great books about that. This example demonstrates the availability of free, great content on the Web and the fact that some of the most qualified people to write a story are bloggers who actually do it for free because … they enjoy it! Most of these people aren't doing it for advertising

revenue or subscription revenue; they are doing it because they want
to be heard. It's not just for news stories either; as we cover later in this
book, it has ramifications on commerce transactions. In a study conducted by Jupiter Research in 2009, it was found that 50 percent of
Internet users consulted a blog prior to making a purchase.[10]

Pundits try to broad brushstroke bloggers and micro-bloggers
(e.g., Twitter, Facebook) as "all bad and uninformed" or "regurgitat-
ing the same news and facts" when in fact there are varying levels of
quality in the blogosphere. Later in this book, we discuss how social
media helps pinpoint the good sources of information from bad ones.
Understandably, these bad-mouthing pundits have a vested interest;
after all, these new outlets are stealing their journalistic jobs.

Not All Bloggers Are Bad

Getting back to World of Mouth, let's continue with this example
to show why the public turns to nontraditional outlets. During this
example, for argument's sake, let's assume that the stories of News
Site A and Blog Site B are exactly the same in terms of quality. There
are three reasons that the Jane the Blogger story has a higher chance
for success than News Site A:

1. She is the most qualified expert on this particular niche subject.
2. She posted first.
3. She has Socialnomics on her side.

The first two are self-explanatory and have been touched on in
other publications, so let's look at the Socialnomics aspect by continuing our story example with Trevor in San Francisco, California.
Trevor is an avid follower of politics, and he has used some social
media tools (e.g., SocialMedian) to alert him once a day about stories
that are related to senators. He receives these two stories (Jane the
Blogger's and News Site A's) in his daily newsfeed via real simple
syndication (RSS) technology. Trevor has no idea how the technology
works, he just knows that his favorite stories show up on his
MyYahoo!, iGoogle, and Facebook home pages. Let's see what happens to each story.

News Site A's Story

Trevor looks at the link for News Site A and likes the catchy title and brief summary of what the story contains. He notices "subscription required" listed next to the link, but he has seen this before and sometimes he is able to get enough of the story. Keep in mind that many readers would have stopped here as soon as they saw "subscription required"—they would not have bothered to click on the hyperlink to the story. However, Trevor is hopeful, clicks through and the page promptly displays a login screen for subscribers only. This is the end of Trevor's experience with News Site A for this particular story and most likely for future stories.

Quick recap of Trevor's experience:

1. He clicks on the headline within his feed for News Site A.
2. He notices "subscription required" for News Site A.
3. The end.

Jane the Blogger's Story

Trevor still wants to read about the drunk-driving senator so he clicks on the next related headline in his feed, which is Jane the Blogger's post. He also sees a link to this same story in his Twitter account. Here's what happens:

1. He clicks on the headline within his feed.
2. He reads and enjoys the story.
3. He posts to his 245 friends on Facebook and 45 followers on Twitter.
4. Forty of his friends/followers read the story.
5. Twenty of his friends/followers who read the story also repost it.
6. Ten of his friends/followers rate and tag it on social media bookmark sites (e.g., Delicious, DIGG, Reddit).
7. A few other web sites and blogs link to this story.
8. Steps 1 through 6 continue in recurring multiples like Russian nesting dolls.

Search engines read these social bookmarks and hyperlinks and rank the article high in their organic rankings for news around the keywords "senator drunk driving." It's important to note that a key aspect of social media is the ability to tag items. In this example, anyone reading the story could add a tag such as "Idaho senator" or "drunk senator," similar in concept to a tag you would use when organizing a manila file folder in a steel filing cabinet. This is done for quick reference later, but it is also extremely helpful in cataloging the Internet for other potential readers. This is instrumental in social media; via tagging, users help other users make sense of all the information available on the Web. (People tell search engines what various pages/articles contain by the tags they apply.) Other forms of tags may include #idahosenators for tools like Twitter.

So, as we mentioned in our opening pages of this book even though social media helps produce more content, it actually causes less confusion and helps make sense of the morass of information on the Web for everyone across the globe. Search engines rightfully look for and aggregate these tags as well as the names of the links to help in ranking items.

Jane the Blogger receives tons of direct traffic from the various direct links to her story. She receives even more traffic from the search engines because so many "voted" for her by social book marking it, reposting it, re-tweets or linking to it. She has thousands of eyes looking at her story that a marketer would be happy to pay decent money for. Her gain is News Site A's loss.

The average person on Facebook has 150 friends—there is a lot of viral potential when one person posts a story or video.

Barriers to entry, like required subscriptions, can cause an unfavorable ripple to cascade into an inevitable crescendo of failure. This example isn't to show that subscription-based news models are a bad thing, although we anticipate by the time you read this book there will be limited subscription-based content models on the Web, but rather it is to indicate that most companies need to fundamentally rethink their business models. The mindset of, "we've always made money this way for the past 100 years, and we are going to stubbornly keep doing it this way" is flawed. Just as flawed is thinking "let's 'digitize' our current offerings but use the same business model" (in this example putting newspaper content online but charging the same subscription price). This model isn't going to work in a time where competitive free Web offerings have similar content. It also hasn't worked as evidenced by Tribune Company filing for bankruptcy at the end of 2008. Tribune is the second largest newspaper conglomerate and has such well-known properties as the *Los Angeles Times* and the *Chicago Tribune.*

We see this type of flawed thinking time after time, and it keeps repeating itself because companies are having a difficult time understanding how to leverage the social graph. Rather than attempt to understand, many forge ahead and try unsuccessfully to impose outdated business models on the social graph. The end result of this type of approach is not pretty.

More progressive thinking is what the *New York Times* has done. They have a monthly subscription based model that automatically downloads to eBook readers like the Amazon Kindle, Sony eReader, Apple iPod, and so on. At the time of this writing, they are charging $12 per month. It is too soon to tell if this type of model will work, but it has a better chance than the models that are attempting to cram a square peg into a round hole. The *New York Times* did a smart thing by looking at the success of Apple iTunes' charging 99 cents per song. There is no need to re-create the wheel if you can just as easily learn from the mistakes and successes of the past. History repeats itself because nobody listens the first time.

There are no physical fees (printing press, web site maintenance, delivery trucks, paper, ink, shipping, and so on) for the *New York Times*, but most importantly it meets the users' desire to have news pushed to them in real time to their preferred mobile device.

Free and Faster Information

Tim Russert was the well-known anchor of the popular television show *Meet the Press* for 17 years. When he unexpectedly passed away in 2008, his *Wikipedia* page was updated before Fox News announced it. The online newspaper-subscription model works well if you are the only one holding the information. However, it breaks down if free and faster information is available. Social media enables this "free and faster" information to exist. Online newspapers would argue that their information is more credible, that *Wikipedia* isn't a reliable source.

While this argument may hold true for smaller niche topics, it's not likely to hold true for the more popular topics. Ironically, major media outlets are designed to cover the big news stories, not the minor niche ones. This makes sense because these niche stories were historically reserved for the local media outlets.

Our major media outlets are now competing against *Wikipedia* and other social collaborative sites, and those sites are stronger. As far back as December 2005, studies were conducted showing the accuracy and viability of *Wikipedia*. One such study was conducted in the journal *Nature* and posted by CNET.

For its study, *Nature* chose articles from both *Encyclopædia Britannica* and *Wikipedia* in a wide range of topics and sent them to what it called "relevant" field experts for peer review. The experts then compared the competing articles side by side —one from each site on a given topic—but were not told which article came from which site. *Nature* collected 42 usable reviews from its field of experts. In the end, the journal found just eight serious errors, such as general misunderstandings of vital concepts, in the articles. Of those, four came from each site.[11]

Think about that, back in 2005, when *Wikipedia* wasn't fully vetted, this study was showing that it was as accurate as *Encyclopædia Britannica*. One could debate (and many have) the validity of this study, but one thing that is very telling is that Britannica itself launched its own version of a Wiki (they need to have final approval) in 2009. Today *Wikipedia* has become even more accurate, not less, due to the increased size and diversity of its contributing user base and increase in editors. *Wikipedia* is bound to be more accurate for major topics—if you have 1,000 experts contributing, versus 3 to 5 experts, the social graph will win every time. However, conversely for niche products, where you have 2 to 3 contributors versus 2 to 3 encyclopedia experts, the experts will provide more reliable information. *Wikipedia* is successful as a result of scale and self-policing. As a result of the success of *Jimmy Wales's Wikipedia* experiment, others have started to leverage the social graph.

One prime example of free and faster information is the site zillow.com. Zillow allows users and realtors to investigate the estimated values of various real estate properties. It aggregates various public data (most recent sale price, up-to-date selling prices of the surrounding houses in the neighborhood, asking prices, quality of schools, etc.) into an algorithm to obtain the estimated property value. To augment this third-party data, Zillow allows its user base to update various aspects. For example, a user can update the number of rooms or bathrooms in a particular home. If you are the homeowner and renovated it by adding a bathroom in the basement, who is a more qualified expert than you (the homeowner) to update the listing?

Google Maps offers a similar wiki functionality by allowing users to move items on the maps so that they are more accurate, such as updating a store that may have gone out of business in the last few weeks. This model works well. Google establishes a baseline product offering (map of the area) and then allows the public to help fine-tune and grow it. This is a slightly different, but just as effective model as *Wikipedia.* The difference is that *Wikipedia* doesn't produce a baseline; rather, everything is developed from scratch.

Wikipedia proves the value of collaboration on a global basis. The output of many minds results in clarity of purpose and innovation. The lesson to be learned is that if collaboration among strangers across the Internet can result in something as useful *Wikipedia*—think about how collaboration among colleagues can transform business.

A Touch of Bacon Salt on Your Social Media

The success of Bacon Salt is a great example of how the social graph can even cause a product to be made. Bacon Salt was an idea that was born out of the minds of two Seattle buddies, Justin Esch and Dave Lefkow, who over a few beers jokingly posed the question— "Wouldn't it be great if there was a powder that made everything taste like bacon?"

The genesis of their success was when Lefkow started a MySpace profile dedicated to Bacon Salt. They then used data openly available on MySpace to seek out people who had mentioned bacon in their profiles—they found over 35,000 such people. They began reaching out to these people to gauge their interest in Bacon Salt, and not only did they find interest, they started receiving orders when they didn't even have a product yet!

World of Mouth took over from there, and as Lefkow describes it, "It was one person telling another person telling another person. It was amazing and scary at the same time. We weren't prepared for the onslaught." The viral aspect of this experience branched into nonsocial media channels, and they even received a free endorsement from the Gotham Girls Roller Derby team. It's one thing to get buzz about your product, it's another thing to sell it—and sell it they did. The spice that made everything taste like bacon incredibly sold 600,000 bottles in 18 months. "We didn't even have a product at the beginning; instead, we bought cheap spice bottles, printed out Bacon Salt logos and scotch taped them onto the bottles."[12]

This product and brand was built entirely using social media. Like JetBlue, Zappos, and Comcast before them, they also started following what people were saying about Bacon Salt and responding to them. They did other activities, but as Lefkow and Esch readily admitted, they wanted to keep some of their social media insights to themselves and indicated "We don't want them (big companies) to get on our gravy train."

Microrevenue Streams Huge for Social Media

The Bacon Salt case study is a good example of a potential revenue stream for the social networks. For a small business owner, it is still very daunting and cumbersome to figure out how to setup a web site for a small business. As evidenced by Lefkow and Esch, you can get a fan page, profile page, group page, and so on up and running on your favorite social network in literally minutes. The best part is, that as of this writing, the social networks don't allow for much customization.

How can noncustomization be a good thing? For small business owners, this places everyone on a level playing field, which means it comes down to the product you're selling versus the glitz and flash of your web site. The functional solution that social networks can provide is the ability to have an automatic shopping cart and transaction model easily established. The social network could take a .005 percent cut of all transactions. This is similar to what Obama excelled at—small payments that add up to millions of dollars. Essentially, this is almost a micropayment model for small businesses. Small businesses can be up and running in a few hours on a social media storefront, and the fractions of pennies that the social media platform captures from transactions would hardly be missed by that small business, but would be a huge revenue generator for the social media platform when they collect from thousands of businesses.

Dancing Matt—Something to Chew On

Later in this book, in more than one example, we show how companies try, some in earnest (TripAdvisor—Where I've Been) and some halfheartedly (Hasbro—Scrabble) to leverage existing successes. These efforts often fall short, and companies wind up developing their own similar marketing programs—sometimes to grand success and other times to failure.

One company that was able to leverage an overnight sensation was chewing gum brand Stride (Cadbury). The story begins with Matthew "Matt" Harding, born September 27, 1976. Harding was an American video game developer from Westport, Connecticut, who had stints at Cutting Edge Entertainment and Activision. Many of these games were primarily *shooter* games. Saying he "didn't want to spend two years of my life writing games about killing everyone," Matt quit his job and began traveling, leading to the production of his first video.

All of us are known for something quirky among our friends, Harding was known for a particular dance. So, while traveling in Vietnam, his travel buddy suggested he do his dance, and they filmed it. The video was uploaded to his web site for friends and family to enjoy, and they loved it! "The dance can probably best be described as a five-year old on a Halloween sugar rush," said Anne McManus of Holland, Michigan.

Harding decided to perform his unique dance whenever he was visiting an exotic location on his journey. He later wound up editing together 15 dance scenes in exotic locations. All the scenes had him center frame, with the background music "Sweet Lullaby."

The video was passed around by e-mail and eventually became *viral,* with Matt's server getting 20,000 or more hits a day as it was discovered generally country by country. The beauty of the video was that there were no language barriers, it was simply Matt dancing in various locations.

Then, once YouTube exploded on the scene, it was a natural fit for Matt to upload it there. Stride Gum saw a huge opportunity and approached Matt, offering to help sponsor his travels. Matt was delighted because he had been traveling on a shoestring budget, actually having to use a college travel company (STA). With the help of Stride, Matt was able to produce a third video in June, 2008.

This video was the result of traveling to 42 different countries over the prior 14 months and included shots from 70 different cities and locations. "It's hard to not smile from watching the video. It really makes you feel good about us one day eventually all being connected globally. With social media I truly think this is possible, and Matt's dancing really is just one example of the power that each of us can unleash," beamed avid YouTube watcher Emmy Spence of Atlanta, Georgia.

One of the founders of YouTube, Jawed Karim, states that Matt's video is his favorite. Karim said that he particularly likes the "Dancing Matt" video because it "illustrates what YouTube is all about—namely that anyone who has a good idea can take that idea and make it happen." Karim said Harding has been hired by a bubble gum company that now pays him to go dance around the world. "Sounds good to me," he said.[13]

This sounds good to Stride gum as well. As of April 2009, over 33 million people had viewed Matt's two most popular videos on YouTube.[14] Keep in mind that this doesn't include all the ancillary videos like "How the Hell Did Matt Get People to Dance with Him?" views), "Where the Hell Is Matt's Girlfriend?" That aggregated also produced a few million views as of April, 2009.

If you typed in "Matt" in Google he shows up for the top 5 results (organic). He was voted a Top 40 Internet Celebrity by VH1, and he made guest appearances on *Good Morning America, The Ellen DeGeneres Show, Jimmy Kimmel Live, Countdown with Keith Olbermann,* just to name a few. For the nominal fee of sponsoring Matt's travel costs, Stride was paid back in millions of dollars worth of brand equity. The best part is the video is still being viewed by the millions, which is completely different from a *one and done* television commercial. In fact as of May, 2009, this video was being showcased on one the premier giant flatscreens in New York's Times Square.

A main reason the campaign was successful was that Stride kept the integrity of the original concept—it was always about people—it wouldn't be prudent to all of a sudden make it about gum. In fact Stride helped Matt improve on his original formula by suggesting that Matt try to surround himself with locals also joining in the dance, whereas previously the somewhat reserved computer programmer would have, at most, one or two people in the video with him. This resulted in some genius results—one of the most inspiring being Matt surrounded in Poria, Papua New Guinea by a tribe (Huli Wigmen) dressed in their indigenous garb. The beauty of this sponsorship is that Matt and his girlfriend Melissa continued to do all of the legwork. Prior to the third video, Matt sent out communications to the various cities he'd be visiting so that he would have people to dance with. He received over 25,000 responses, and he needed to get release forms signed prior to the filming. This is quite a bit of legwork that could easily get bogged down in the legal department of a large corporation. In this instance, Matt and his girlfriend were continuing to produce the videos from point A to point Z.

Stride could have had Matt wearing a Stride T-shirt and passing out gum, but they were smart enough to leave well enough alone. Instead, they had a tactful message at the end of the video (i.e., post roll) and also had a discreet logo in the upper right of some of the videos. Stride showed how successful a brand can be by simply associating itself with social media that is already virally successful, which gives other brands something to chew on.

Flying the Not-So-Friendly Skies

A good example of the *viralness* of social media can be seen in this American Airlines example. In April of 2008, over the course of four days, American Airlines had to cancel 3,000 flights as a result of a large percentage of their jets' not meeting the maintenance requirements mandated by the Federal Aviation Administration. This was not the result of bad weather or security threats; it was pure negligence on the part of American Airlines. A spokesman for American Airlines expressed their strategy in handling the situation:

> We fly over 100 million passengers a year, and they are all important to us. A large percentage of them fly with us exclusively, so the most important goal was to stay in contact and let them know what was going on. And we used *every communications channel* we have available to us.
>
> This included some new plays, including monitoring blogs, as soon as the crisis started. That was an important part of our strategy. And we felt, in general, that the information was generally correct and balanced enough to where *we didn't have to get involved in the conversation.* Some of the remarks were tough to take and on some blogs people were actually defending us.[15]

I underline two important pieces in this statement. The first is that "we used every communication channel available to us," yet there is no specific mention of social media. The second is "we didn't have to get involved with the conversation." As an individual or company, you should feel compelled to become part of the conversation, people want to be heard. A strategy of we will only enter a conversation if it "gets ugly" is generally flawed logic in the sense that the damage will be done before you can react. This is similar to trying to time the stock market; very difficult.

Web site complaints to www.aa.com increased 25 percent over the same period the year before and 9 percent over the previous week.[16] American asked consumers with complaints about the cancellations and inconveniences to e-mail them. This caused a 13 percent increase in e-mail complaints. What jumped out was a 74 percent increase in downstream traffic to social network MySpace.[17] This is compelling in the sense that users were most likely going to social media to vent and widely disseminate their own personal issues with the crisis. This large increase couldn't only be caused by teens because teens index low on travel volume. Also, as noted in the previous quote, there was no mention of specifically monitoring social media outlets—only blogs. This type of rabid activity on social media can affect an airline's brand equity, yet as stated by the American Airlines spokesman, they weren't using the popular social media tools, listening to what was being said, and attempting to address it. They chose to ignore these important conversations. Later in this book, we will show how JetBlue has correctly taken the appropriate measures to make sure they are listening and responding within social media to disgruntled consumers. Will American Airlines listen?

Chapter One Key Points

1. Despite niche fragmentation caused by the Internet, people still desire an understanding of what the majority is doing. Social media is that mechanism.

2. Wasting time on social media actually makes you more productive. Social media is the mechanism that allows users to avoid "information indigestion." Recall the Sally Supermarket example where she uses social media to turn 10 minutes of historically wasted time into 10 productive and enjoyable minutes.

3. Business models need to shift. Simply digitizing old business models doesn't work; businesses need to fully transform to properly address the impact and demands of social media.

4. Traditional magazines and newspapers are struggling for online survival because some of the most qualified people to write a story are freelance bloggers who write for the sheer

joy of it! They aren't writing in hopes of subscription revenue; they are posting free content (opinions, videos, facts,
etc.) because they want to be heard. It's tough for traditional
journalists and publications to compete with the free and
good model of blogs.

5. In the future, we will no longer look for the news; rather, the
   news will find us or we will create it. That future is now.

6. A key aspect of social media is the ability for millions to tag
   items just like you would label a manila folder. This helps
   catalog the information on the Web and makes it easier for
   all users.

7. Not all great viral marketing ideas need to originate in the
   marketing department. It is prudent to team up with already
   successful grassroots programs (e.g., Stride Gum and
   Dancing Matt).

Chapter Two

Social Media = Preventative Behavior

We've covered, hopefully at an entertaining and lucid level, why there is such a thirst and demand for social media, but what does social media demand from us? While millions of people have discovered the benefits of social media, some people and companies have also experienced the potential pitfalls of such mass transparency.

More than a few students have been kicked out of universities for collaborating on Twitter, hi5, Facebook, MySpace, and the like for assigned individual school projects. It's old news that potential employers haven't hired some people purely because of inappropriate content or associations on their MySpace or Facebook pages. Or, how about the teachers who have been asked to step down for overtly sexual content within their social networks. There's also the famous Jeff Jarvis blog post about Dell's inadequate customer service.

So what does this all mean? Are social networks powerful enough to cause an adjustment in personal and corporate behavior on a macrolevel? You bet your camera phone they are.

The 20-something now thinks twice about getting so drunk that she blacks out and can't remember how she wound up in the hammock of a stranger's backyard. Cameras document everything, and technologies like Facebook's Mobile Upload and "tagging" can disseminate a naked keg stand to your network faster than you can count to five.

Sure, many still have the desire to put their deepest and darkest thoughts and behaviors into a black box, but they are less likely to be able to keep their actions secret.

Staying in Touch with Your Teenagers

When you get home from a hard day at work and ask your kids what happened in school, many respond with the same answer that you did when you were a teenager—"nothing." They aren't intentionally being difficult (at least most of the time); they are just teenagers being teenagers. They do not understand that the fact that their classmates Holly and Suzy were pulling each other's hair in gym class is incredibly intriguing. Or, the fact that the substitute teacher went an entire class period not knowing she had toilet paper on her shoe would provide much needed levity to a parent returning from a stressful or monotonous day at the office.

In many instances, social media can help bring families a little closer by enabling parents to unobtrusively follow their kids' lives. At best, parents and teenagers share time around the dinner table, and then everyone goes about his or her own life. To some extent, social media changes this dynamic—it connects parents to their kids like never before. "I think one of the real beauties of social media is the passivity of it. Unlike e-mail that requires a response, a mother or grandmother can passively observe the whereabouts and activities of their children or grandchildren," indicates Steve Kaufer, CEO of TripAdvisor.

While ignorance can sometimes be bliss, social media provides insight for parents into the day-to-day activities of their children. But you shake your head and say there is no way that kids would allow their parents to spy like that. You would be right, but it's not universally true. Although some junior high students don't mind being seen with their parents at the movies, others would rather be dead than be spotted with their parents in public. Also keep in mind that some parents will not bless their children's social media usage unless they are also part of their child's network.

Obviously, if their parents are in the social network, then teenagers will be taking on preventative behaviors. Keep in mind that teenagers will also take on preventative behaviors not only for their parents, but also for some of their classmates. For example, if a rowdy, partying guy was trying to impress a particularly prudish and reserved girl—

his behavior in the social network might be a little more refined after she becomes a part of his network and is privy to his activities and behavior.

Preventative Behavior for Business

The great thing about technologies like microblogging (Twitter, FriendFeed, Six Apart) for businesses is that there are tools that enable you to type in your brand name like "Hershey" or "Prada" and see what millions are talking about. Good companies do this, but savvy companies take it one step further and act on it.

Comcast, who has notoriously terrible customer service, did a progressive and great thing from the beginning when it came to microblogging. Comcast assigned a person to monitor conversations for any mention of the term "Comcast," and more important, they also gave that company representative the authority to respond and act. This first came to the public's attention when famous blogger Michael Arrington of TechCrunch had his service down for over 36 hours and was getting no help from customer service over the phone. He ranted on Twitter about how much he despised Comcast's service, and pals like Jeff Jarvis ("Dell Hell") started reposting the story. To Arrington's surprise, he was contacted within 20 minutes by a Comcast representative who was following rants on Twitter, and his issue was resolved by the next day. Another example of Comcast's progressiveness was posted by C. C. Chapman on the blog "Managing the Gray":

> I just had an amazing experience in customer service from Comcast.... With all the flack they have gotten over the years, I've actually been very fortunate to have a mostly good experience with them and the last 24 hours really proves that when a brand pays attention to the conversation happening out on the web about them and actively works to engage in that, good things can happen.
>
> ... last night I made a snide remark about the lackluster quality of my HD picture on Comcast during the Celtics game. Comcast saw that and tweeted me back minutes later. This morning I got a call from their service center. This afternoon

someone came out. Now my HDTV rocks! THAT my friends is customer service and how it should work all the time.

Brands need to wake up to the fact that "new media" isn't going away and in fact, I'd argue that it isn't new anymore, but is here and at the forefront so you either wake up and pay attention or you lose business to the company that is paying attention.[1]

JetBlue also engaged in trying to keep a pulse on its customers. When a company starts to follow you on Twitter or another microblog, it may seem a little too Big Brother-like, but if the company is transparent, then the consumer's concerns about too much information sharing go away. For example this is a typical response from JetBlue:

Sorry if we weirded you out by following you on Twitter. @JetBlue isn't a bot, it's merely me and my team keeping our ears to the ground and listening to our customers talk in open forums so we can improve our service. It's not marketing, it's trying to engage on a level other than mass broadcast, something I personally believe more companies should try to do.

Because corporate involvement in social media is a new and evolving discipline, I also take a specific interest in conversations revolving around our role here. I'd have messaged you directly if you allowed direct messages, so please also forgive me for following the link on your twitter page here to send you this note.

You and Lisa are no longer being "followed" as you indicate. Again, my apologies.

Morgan Johnston
Corporate Communications
JetBlue Airways[2]

Notice what Morgan says, "It's not marketing, it's trying to engage on a level other than mass broadcast."

Authors are constantly doing vanity searches on Twitter search to determine if people are talking about them or about their book. One author says, "I was doing a vanity search on my name within Twitter when I saw a post out of Billings, Montana, that had happened in the last two minutes and the exchange went something like this."

Author: My husband just handed me a book by Tim Ash called *Landing Page Optimization.* Is this any good?

Tim Ash: Yes, it's a great book.

Author: Aren't you the author?

Tim Ash: Yes, I am.

Author: Well, if I don't like this book will you refund my money?

Tim Ash: Yes, I'm so confident that you will like the book that I will refund your money if you don't.

As you read this, you may say wait, this isn't necessarily new, good companies have been responding to comments on message boards for several years now, especially after popular blogger Jeff Jarvis flamed (no pun intended) Dell in his "Dell Hell" post in 2005.[3]

The concept of responding to customer unhappiness is certainly not new and not new on the Web. The difference with social media is the speed and ease in which this occurs as well as the sphere of influence.

A post on a message board can take a company quite some time to find (i.e., time measured in days), if they find it at all. This can also be a labor intensive and costly process for companies to follow. The key problem is that it is often very labor intensive for the user to post a complaint. To post on a message board, you generally are required to set up an account for that particular message board. Message boards are sometimes difficult to navigate to a particular topic area, and so on.

In the past, millions of frustrated customers didn't bother to comment or let a company know their frustration. Now, it is so easy to disseminate information from anywhere (in particular from your mobile device) that more and more customers are doing it. With programs like Facebook Connect and Friend Connect (Google), now one can use an easy-to-remember login (Facebook or Google) no matter what site you happen to be on, whether it's cnet.com or cbssportline.com.

With social media tools, you can post a comment/video in seconds directly from your laptop or most likely your mobile device. This is critical because it allows frustrated customers to instantly post their exact feeling at the point of frustration. They haven't had time to ruminate, so it is unbridled. Similarly, the posts are easy for companies like JetBlue and Comcast to see. It's not laborious at all to find problems, in fact they can assign one person to help handle most situations, which means they have more time to focus on the solution rather than spending time finding the problem.

This gets to another point on how great companies philosophically approach critically posted content on the Web. Ineffective companies that aren't in touch with their customers, view negative posts as a nuisance because it takes time to figure out how to technically scrub or manipulate them by means of posting bogus "good" user comments or applying pressure to the site(s) via antitrademark infringement laws to remove the post.

Effective companies and people relish critical online feedback. They use this information to make themselves more competitive by improving their products and services in the eyes of the consumer. These companies don't waste their time attempting to manipulate online systems; rather, they spend their time (like in the JetBlue Twitter example) trying to resolve the issue with the disgruntled customer and learning from it. Good companies view it as an opportunity to prove to that customer they are willing to go the extra mile for them.

A good everyday analogy of constructive feedback is a friend who lets you know when you have an unsightly poppy seed stuck in your teeth prior to a big blind date. This friend is much more valuable to you than the politically polite and silent friend. Perhaps the biggest difference between these examples and traditional message boards doesn't have anything to do with the tactical or the technology. It has to do with the sphere of influence of the person posting.

If the fictitious Peter Poster places something on a message board, he doesn't know who he is reaching, and the reader most likely doesn't know who Peter is. With social media, Peter posts a status update on Facebook, LinkedIn, Twitter, etc. This status update is sent to people within his network who all (personally) know him. By knowing Peter, they can readily identify with the position Peter is coming from.

If Peter complains about a Boston creme doughnut from a particular bakery, his followers may discredit it and say "That Peter is always so fickle when it comes to eating, it's rare if he likes any food item that his mother doesn't make." Conversely, if Peter complains about the poor customer response from a phone provider, a follower may say, "When it comes to eating, Peter is fickle, but he is very patient and forgiving otherwise, so if he says his phone company has poor customer service, I'm going to make certain that I steer clear of that phone company."

> Someone who has stayed only at five-star hotels will rate a five-star hotel differently than a honeymooner staying at a five-star for the first time.
> —Bill Tancer, General Manager, Global Research, Hitwise

One step would be to find someone you don't know on general review sites who seems to have similar tastes; however, the next logical and more rewarding approach is locating a person in your social network who you know and who you are confident (via personal knowledge) has the same preferences you do.

Let's perform a quick calculation based on the average number of people that a person on Twitter has following them to underscore the importance of social media. The old rule of thumb was that a person who had a bad experience would tell 6 to 10 people about it. The average person on Twitter follows 100 people. If you take that and assume that 10 percent of the people following someone will pass it along, then you get to the number 10 ($100 \times 0.10 = 10$). Ten people will be influenced directly. If those 10 also have 100 followers and only 5 percent pick it up, then another 50 individuals will be influenced indirectly, and so it goes on down the line. That's quite an impact.

Chapter Two Key Points

1. Businesses and people are willing to have open diaries within social media as a way to stay connected because their ultimate desire is to feel a part of something larger than themselves. With this openness comes responsibility for both businesses and individuals.

2. What happens in Vegas stays on YouTube.

3. Individuals and companies are starting to lead their lives as if their mother or board of directors were watching their every move because they probably are. While there are downsides to these behavioral changes caused by social media, overall it's beneficial to society.

4. Social media connects parents to their kids like never before.

5. Social media enables frustrated customers to instantly post their unbridled frustrations.

6. Negative comments and posts are easier for companies to find with social media. Hence those companies have more time to focus on the solution rather than spending time finding the problem.

7. Effective companies and people relish critical feedback via social media. Customer comments that identify areas for improvement are invaluable.

8. Poor companies spend time attempting to obfuscate or manipulate negative comments within social media. Good companies spend time addressing and resolving customer complaints.

Chapter Three

Social Media = Braggadocian Behavior

The second, more exciting change is braggadocian behavior. As people continue to microblog, and update their status via social media, it soon becomes a competition of who's doing the coolest thing. What once took place only periodically around the watercooler is now happening in real time.

Would you rather post "I'm watching reruns of *Saved By the Bell*" or post "Just snowboarded down a double-black diamond run at Aspen and highly recommend it for those who love Colorado snow!" Over time, each of these posts contributes to *your* individual brand.

As a society, this is a good thing. It allows people to take stock of their collective lives and what they're doing throughout the day, rather than letting years go by and looking back on their wasted youth, saying "what did I do with my life?"

Is it any wonder that the television audience is shrinking by the minute? People are actually living their own lives rather than watching others. As a company, it's imperative that you produce products and services so that people not only want to be associated with your brand, but also take ownership of it.

Social Media Is In

Out: Reality TV

In: Reality social media

Just Do It, Did It

Nike understood how to take advantage of users' appetites for competition as well as users looking to brands for helpful tools (creators of content). That is why Nike created an avatar named Miles that people can place on their desktops. Miles helps users by tracking the miles they run or their jogging patterns (via Nike Plus technology) compared to others inside and outside of their network. Miles encourages you to run and keeps you aware of local weather, running events, and promotions. This can easily be used wherever you are (iPod, social network, desktop, etc.).

Companies need to focus on giving content or a tool with utility and purpose to consumers, which is the opposite of traditional marketing, which consumers historically hated. Instead of providing end consumers with a potentially empty promise, as was the case with traditional marketing, companies need to focus on supplying something of value. People are grateful that Nike is able to provide them with a tool to track how many miles they run and to tell them which songs from their iPod playlists seem to stimulate them to run their best. Allowing users to see what songs stimulate other runners, which may include tunes that are not currently in their iPod repertoire, is a tremendous help.

This social media technique also helps align Nike and Apple with additional revenue because more songs will be downloaded and more shoes will wear out and need to be replaced. Plus, every time a person's running profile is updated, it will be sent to that person's entire network of friends with Nike branding discreetly associated with it. In fact, joggers are encouraged to challenge others to virtual races in which their respective performances are tracked via the tracking technology placed in the shoes.

Other stationary spinning and bicycle manufacturers have picked up on the social aspect of exercising and the ability to enable connections via social media technology. Some of these bikes that have a built-in LCD and Web connection allow Joe in his gym in New York to compete against Sally in her spa in Santa Fe. Looking at the digital screen you see real-time avatars of others cycling across the world and you can pass or be passed. This also allows for the introduction of celebrity athletes; yes, you could be virtually competing against Lance

Armstrong. This is a huge opportunity for advertisers that could sponsor the Lance avatar or could even sponsor Joc from New York if he became the most proficient within the virtual racing world.

Social Media Is the New Inbox

The "killer" tool of the first part of the Internet boom was e-mail, and then along came e-commerce, e-care, search, music, video, and now social media. E-mail has held on through the years as, arguably, the king of the Internet, used by the old and the young. However, the new Inbox is shifting toward social media.

"I have a sixteen-year-old cousin, and she listed her favorite web sites and applications and failed to mention e-mail, so I asked her about it. I was shocked by the incredulous look on her face and even more shocked at her response that she didn't use e-mail that much since it was too formal; she would rather use instant messenger on her phone or post comments based on people's activities in social networks," said Mike Peters, 37, of Detroit, Michigan. It turns out that Generations Y and Z finds e-mail antiquated and passé, so they simply ignore it.

While this is shocking to some generations, it fits within the scheme of Socialnomics. E-mail isn't entirely going away; it just may not be the first means of digital communication in a Socialnomic world. Messaging is much easier to manage within social media versus e-mail because it acts like a real conversation among friends.

"As a salesperson, I see social networks like LinkedIn and Facebook as invaluable tools. It doesn't necessarily shorten the sales cycle, but what it does is keep the information flow more open and also allows for a much deeper relationship than e-mail. I've started relationships and signed contracts exclusively within social networks. It is revolutionary for sales, it's much easier than telephone calls and e-mails," said Allison Bahm of Response Mine Interactive Agency.

Whereas e-mail functions in a nonfluid manner:

"How are you doing?"

"Fine."

Open conversations within social media have an easier flow to them and replicate a normal conversation. Also, the conversational content is broken down into bite-size chunks and is associated into more easily recognized compartments rather than just a long and daunting slew of 45 e-mails that you need to wade through systematically.

> Kids today prefer one-to-many communication; e-mail
> to them is antiquated.
> —Bill Tancer, General Manager, Global Research,
> Hitwise

People are updating their status: "I'm depressed," or "I got a new job," and it is much easier to read this and stay connected than to send a series of e-mails asking how someone is doing or what that person is up to. In a sign of the times ahead and for the first time since e-mail was invented, Boston College will not be giving out @bc.edu e-mail addresses to incoming freshmen for the class of 2013.

"At Apple, we generally hire early adopters. That being said, I was still blown away when we recently hired a 22-year-old and he had literally never sent an e-mail. Via his iPhone he had always communicated with his friends either by instant messenger, text, phone call, or comments within Facebook. I believe he is not alone and this is a trend we will continue to see with the next generation," said a director of Apple iTunes .

"Are You on Facebook?" Is the New "Can I Get Your Phone Number?"

The most underlying factor for this new inbox may be the seismic shift in the way people exchange information. Let's take a quick look at the evolution of dating over the past 10 years. First, people used to give out their home phone number. Then people began to give out their e-mail address instead.

At first it seemed odd to ask someone for a date over e-mail, but then it became quite natural. Then we progressed to mobile phone numbers because some people didn't have landlines anymore. Besides, it was easier to text message each another—it was less intrusive and awkward: "What are you doing tonight?"

Today with social media, when people meet, it's common for one of them to ask the other person, "Are you on hi5?" "Are you on Facebook?" or "Tu estas en Orkut?" Just as people use the word Google as a verb—google it—they are starting to use phrases like "Facebook me or send me a Tweet" People are no longer exchanging e-mails, they are exchanging each other's social media information. In many instances, people would never give out their e-mail addresses, and if they desired that type of communication, social networks have inboxes of their own that replicate and replace e-mail.

Executives are still holding hard and fast to the concept of the traditional inbox. In a survey of 180 Chief Marketing Officers of $1 billion corporations that was conducted by GfK Roper Public Affairs and Media, they found that while 70 percent were decreasing their marketing budgets, the area in which they were least likely to make cuts was e-mail.[1] You can't necessarily blame them for this type of thinking. This has been one of their best performing channels for years, and they've spent money building and managing their databases.

Now and in the future, marketers need to adjust their way of thinking because it's no longer about building out the existing database. Instead, you could be in communication with fans and consumers on someone else's database (Facebook, YouTube, Twitter, etc.). Yet, many companies fail to grasp this new concept. They build elaborate YouTube or Flicker pages, placing callouts and click actions that send the user outside the social network, often to their company web site or a lead capture page. These companies still believe they need to get users into their prospecting databases in order to market to them. They are doing a disservice to their loyal fan base and in turn a disservice to themselves.

It's analogous to meeting a pretty girl in a bar and asking if she would like a drink. When she responds "yes," rather than ordering a drink from the bartender, you grab her and rush her into your car and drive her back to your place; because after all, you have beer in your fridge. This is not a sound courtship strategy, nor should companies employ comparable social media strategies in "courting" potential customers. It is best to be patient rather than to rush into things, without consumer confidence; just like in dating, you have nothing without it.

Deep Dive into Dating 101

Let's digress back to our dating scenario on social media. Social networks are fantastic for meeting new people and dating. If a girl meets a guy out on the town and they exchange names and connect within a social media network—it's a gold mine of data.

The more friends you have in common within a shared social network, the more secure you feel knowing the other person isn't some form of lunatic. Photos are helpful, especially if the night before was a bit wild and a little fuzzy. If you are listed in a network for "Star Trek Fanatics" or "Dracula Oprah" that will be even more telling about who you really are. What you do, who you work for, where you live and have lived, provides additional insight into your personality.

If all checks out fine, that first date is more like a fourth date, you aren't asking question like "Where did you go to college?" or "What are your hobbies?" It's somewhat sad, but true. You will still probably ask these questions so that it won't appear that you are a stalker or to show a polite interest, but it is a completely different dynamic than the world baby boomers, or even Generation Xers, grew up in. Social networks make it easier to stay in touch with someone new before you are at the "Let's grab a drink" stage. It's easier than face-to-face because you avoid awkward silences, don't have to worry about who is going to pay the check, and don't experience potentially embarrassing situations (poppy seed between the teeth anyone?).

Already gaining popularity on the dating side of things is leveraging the mobility of having alerts sent to your phone so that you are connected to people who are currently in your area. Going one step further, some tools recommend locations based on your mood. Instead of listing the top-10 restaurants in the SoHo area of New York, it lists the top-10 romantic restaurants or the top-20 hip, laid-back restaurants; so, if it was your first date, it wouldn't be awkward being at a place with white-glove service and dining by candlelight.

The benefits of this type of relationship building hold true from business to consumer as well. Businesses capture more information via social media about their consumers than they've ever had before. Good businesses realize that the relationship still needs to be cultivated (see the grabbing the girl from the bar analogy). Good businesses realize that it's not all about the instant win of getting someone into a database. Rather it is cultivating that relationship via social media. If it's done correctly, you will have a relationship that lasts a lifetime.

Assess Your Life Every Minute

The examples presented in this section stress a crucial maxim of this book. Social media allows individuals to take real-time inventories of their lives and help answer the age-old question "What am I doing with my life?"

Bill, 82, says,

> I actually made a habit of physically printing out my social media updates from the previous month and going through them one by one and highlighting updates that weren't necessarily contributing to a "full" life. Over time, I reduced the amount of "waste" and actually became so cognizant of it during the actual act of updating my stats that I'd recognize in that specific moment in time what I would deem an "unfruitful activity" and cease engaging in it immediately. My life is much more fulfilling because of this! I wish these social media tools were around a long time ago![2]

Heather, a mother of three, has her own story about how social media is helping her lead a more productive life:

> I had a close friend who was married without children. One day she confided in me that she didn't know if she was ready for children. She thought she was but then she mentioned something that floored me; the conversation went something like this:

> "Heather, I'm just not sure that I'm up for it, I mean you are

probably the most with-it person that I know and it seems like your kids are all that you can handle."

To which I responded, "Yes, having kids is life-changing and presents its new challenges, but it's not as bad as people let on; for every one thing my kids do bad, they do nine things that light up my life."

"Really? That's good news to hear and helps alleviate some of my concerns, but to be blunt, it's also a little surprising given the social media status updates I receive from you."

I was obviously surprised to hear this revelation from one of my closest friends, and I didn't think it had much validity. So, later that day, I wanted to prove it was unwarranted. I pulled up the last several weeks of updates, which didn't take me too long since I only did one or two updates per day. There it was staring back me in black and white; my friend was exactly right! While my kids were the greatest joy in my life, you would never know it from reading my updates. My kids provided 90 percent of all the new wonders and happiness in my life, yet I was conveying the exact opposite in my status updates. For every one positive status update about my kids, "Lilly gives the best hugs" or "I posted Will's beautiful finger painting on the fridge," I'd post nine negative ones, "Have a massive headache from the kids nonstop screaming" or "Not sure I can handle a full day at the zoo with the kids again."

The reality of the situation shocked me, and I was fearful that there was a possibility that I was also projecting this negative attitude onto the kids. The answer to this came sooner than expected. For the next few weeks, I made a concerted effort not to post anything remotely negative on the social media platforms I used. Or at least have it reflect my reality, nine positive posts for every single negative post. Then one day, about two weeks into practicing this experience, it really hit home when my four-year-old tugged at my shirt and looked up at me with her big blue eyes and said, "Mommy, you seem a lot more happy, and I really like it."[3]

Updating your status or microblogging about what you are doing are immediate reminders of exactly that! And, if you pause, like Bill, and look back over a day, week, or month of what you posted, it is extremely enlightening because it shows you how you are spending what precious time you have.

Millennials —All About Giving Back

In 2008, Millennials (Generation Yers) showed up in record numbers to vote. In comparison, record numbers of jaded Generation Xers never stepped out to vote when they were in their early 20s, despite all the Rock the Vote hoopla on MTV at the time.[4]

In 2008, the most popular Facebook application wasn't a fancy game, music, or TV show. It was an application called "Causes" with almost 20 million active monthly uses.[5] The application was quite simple in its description: Causes lets you start and join the causes you care about. Donations to Causes can benefit over a million registered nonprofit organizations. Not surprisingly, this was a far cry from the 1980's "Me Generation." Recall that one of the popular songs of that era was Madonna's "Living in a Material World."

Generation Yers grew up in the 1980s, and after witnessing the horror that can be caused by narcissistic behavior, they wanted to do everything in their power to be the opposite of that. Their kids aren't going to grow up as latchkey kids. The social community aspect simply doesn't stop at discussing the hottest young pop star. No, Generation Y has a strong sense for making the world a better place.

While the majority of this book stresses the many positive aspects of social media, we'd be misleading if we did not highlight the downside as well. One trend we are starting to see is Generation Y and Z's difficulty with face-to-face interactions.

The Next Generation Can't Speak

The desire and ability to meet new people has rapidly eroded so much so that humans fear public speaking more than death. This led comedian Jerry Seinfeld to quip, "According to surveys on what we fear ... you are telling me that at a funereal, most people would rather be the guy in the coffin than have to stand up and give the eulogy?"[6]

Difficult and awkward subjects are much easier to deal with hiding behind instant messaging or social media comments than face-to-face.

And even written skills have eroded from living in a 140-character world.

A study by the nonprofit group that administers the SAT and other placement tests (National Commission on Writing at the College Board) found:

- 50 percent of teens surveyed say they sometimes fail to use proper capitalization and punctuation in assignments.
- 38 percent have carried over IM or e-mail shortcuts such as LOL.
- 25 percent of teens have used :) and other emoticons.
- 64 percent have used at least one of the informational elements in school.[7]

So, yes there are downsides to not having as much face-to-face interaction and that's a challenge these two generations and future generations face because technology is an intrinsic part of their lives, but the positive aspects are plentiful. They have an understanding of their place in the global community and are more creative and collaborative. They don't mind challenging the status quo—which is much different than simply not respecting it. They expect a better work-life balance, are better at prioritization and multitasking. They need more guidance in management skills, project planning, and business communication.

They are less likely to understand boundaries whether that is answering e-mail from a friend during business hours or taking e-mail from a manager at 11 PM. To them, things are just more fluid; it's not a 9-to-5 world, it's a 24/7 world, and it's up to the individual to properly balance the hours in the day. Generation Xers and Yers think it's laughable that a company would block Facebook or YouTube during work hours—you are either getting the job done or you are not getting the job done. Workers realize that if they play during the workweek they will have to work on Saturday to complete the necessary tasks. But that is a conscious decision they make.

Let Kids Take Ownership of Your Brand

"Young Adults Revealed" global survey conducted by Synovate in partnership with Microsoft was designed to find out how much young adults interact and engage online with brands on a daily basis. The research included 12,603 people 18 to 24 years old from 26 countries. The survey revealed that 28 percent say they talked about a brand on a discussion forum, 23 percent added brand related content to their IM service, and 19 percent added branded content to their homepage or favorite social sites.[8]

The research concluded that young adults are more than willing to add brand content to their instant messenger services, Web homepages, and social networking sites. The researchers found the survey respondents spent an average of 2.5 hours online daily in nonwork-related activity. Synovate's global manager of syndicated research, Julian Rolfe indicates,

> The research shows that young people are not only comfortable with the idea of branded content and branded entertainment, but also reveals they are openly willing and eager to engage online with brands.
>
> They clearly feel their opinions about brands are important, they want to associate themselves with brands they see as "cool" and this is why we see them uploading clips to their social networking sites and IM services.[9]

Synovate found that one in ten said they passed along viral ads and marketing clips.[10] For brand marketers, this should be welcome news, your consumer wants to have a relationship with you and even help out where they can. All it takes is honesty, transparency, listening, and reacting. Because not every company can do these well, the ones that do will win decisively.

Kids Ages 2 to 17 Don't See Advertisements

A 2008 Nielsen study found that kids ages 2 to 11 endure the least amount of advertisements on the Internet. The group experiencing the second lowest ad exposure is the next age group in succession (12 to

17). The amount of ads someone was exposed to was somewhat correlated with age, as the 65 and older demographic sees the most ads.[11]

This speaks to the infancy of social media because this is where a lot of teens spend the majority of their time. It also speaks to the fact that the social media companies realize that theirs is not a place to attempt to "force fit" an old advertising model into a completely new and different space; insert square peg into round hole here. The limited ad exposure of kids under 12 years of age is due in part to protection laws coupled with the fact that many of the more popular kids' sites (e.g., Webkinz) carry few, if any, advertisements.

The upside to this as a marketer is that if you are able to integrate your content (note we say content rather than advertising), then it will stand out even more because there is less clutter.

Turning Lemons into Lemonade with Fizzle

A salient example of companies less steered by their legal department is the Diet Coke and Mentos experiment. This started with two scientists experimenting in a laboratory one day and discovering that if you dropped five Mentos (chewable gum-like candy with a hard outer shell) into Diet Coke, a fairly volatile chemical reaction would ensue. They perfected these geysers and determined that five Mentos on a fishing line dropped into a two-liter of Diet Coke with the cap on and a tiny hole at the top would result in the most dramatic effect.

Since it was so visual and dynamic, YouTube was the perfect platform to make it globally famous. Before the existence of a social media site like YouTube, only a select few in the science community would have known about it. In the past, the Coca-Cola Company could possibly have handled this quietly behind closed doors; however, in today's world with the heightened social media exposure, Coke was forced to deal with the situation. Let's look at how they handled it.

In the past, Coke would have been alarmed by this discovery. There was also probably good cause for this potential alarm because the public could jump to the incorrect assumption that Coke must be highly toxic and it would be undesirable to have this type of reaction going on in the stomach. The end result would have most likely been a long court battle by Coke to discredit and shut these activities down.

The social media exposure and blog reporting today don't allow for events/news to be handled discreetly anymore. Equally important for Coke to consider was the competition. The scientists, Fritz Grobe (the short one) and Stephen Voltz (the tall one) through their testing discovered that the best results came from using Diet Coke. Sprite, Diet Pepsi, Coke Classic, and Dr. Pepper didn't produce the same dramatic effect with Mentos. While it wasn't as dramatic an effect, these other sodas still produced a spectacular result.

Hence a window was open for Pepsi to do something if Coke didn't (the mindset that if you don't do something, someone else will). Pepsi could have shown that their products didn't have the same explosive reaction and compared themselves side-by-side with Coke using a proactive question of "which would you rather have in your kids' stomach?"

Weighing these factors, as well as other World of Mouth ramifications, Coke decided to embrace the exposure of this experiment and actually hired Grobe and Fritz as spokesman. They in turn went on to do a much more elaborate video on YouTube that won Coke many marketing awards and has resulted to date in over 9 million views on YouTube. The transparency and exposure of social media is having the positive effect of companies starting to embrace items that they historically would have either ignored (in hopes they'd go away) or not implement for fear of legal liability or backlash.

If a company or individual has something to brag about now or in the future, we will see that they are going to let the world know through every social media tool available. The great thing is that if they don't have anything to brag about, then they will alter their behavior (e.g., watching TV) to something more interesting (e.g., writing a screenplay), which in turn has them contributing more and more to improving society as a whole.

Chapter Three Key Points

1. Social media allows individuals to take real-time inventories of their lives and helps answer the age-old question "What

am I doing with my life?" This benefits society because it encourages more people to engage in productive or charitable activities.

2. Reality TV has been replaced by reality social media—it's all about my friends and my own reality.

3. Social media is the new inbox: Younger generations find e-mail antiquated and passé.

4. Generations Y and Z interpersonal communication skills have been retarded by reliance on social media tools that aren't face-to-face or verbal.

5. Generations Y and Z have a desire to contribute to the greater world around them and leverage social media for social and charitable causes.

Chapter Four

Social Media Delivers Obama the White House

John F. Kennedy was helped into the White House by the increasing popularity of a new medium, television. The same can be said about our current President, Barack Obama. He was also greatly helped by a new medium, but it was social media. Within minutes of Colin Powell's endorsement of Obama on October 19, it was posted on the Web. As mentioned throughout this book, this presidential election quickly forced traditional broadcasters on ABC, NBC, CBS, and so on to adjust how they covered election news, otherwise people would find content elsewhere (YouTube, Wikipedia, blogs, podcasts, etc.). After Powell's endorsement on NBC's *Meet the Press,* NBC had the announcement ready to go on its sister property, msnbc.com.

NBC was also wise enough to post the video to the Web before the West Coast was able to see the interview on traditional television. It is essential that traditional broadcasters embrace socialnomics; otherwise, they will be overrun into oblivion. People use several media sources in combination to formulate an opinion—not just one source. Networks that recognize this and attempt to work effectively with the new forms of social media will survive.

"We should be careful of these zero-sum games where the new media drives out the old," said Andrew Heyward, a former president of CBS News who consults for the Monitor Group. "I think what we see is growing sophistication about making the channels work together effectively."[1]

Perhaps due to his widespread appeal to younger audiences, but more likely due to limited funding at the outset of his campaign, Obama embraced social media from the beginning—knowing that he had a chance to dominate this medium over his Democratic opponents. Attempting to dominate traditional media (newspapers, television, radio) would have been a tactical error against his well-known opponent, Hillary Clinton, and more important, the Clinton Political Machine. Because of the hard-fought battle with Hillary, Obama was well positioned from a social media position when he won the Democratic nomination and entered the presidential race.

His followers and supporters from a social media perspective, weren't going to go away, rather they were going to grow substantially and contribute in record sums—with $5 and $10 donations quickly adding up to a multimillion-dollar arsenal.

By the time Obama was elected, he had over 3.1 million fans on his Facebook fan age. This number didn't include the various other Fan Pages and Groups like "Students for Obama," "Pride for Obama," "Michelle Obama," "Florida for Obama," "Michigan for Obama," "Pennsylvania for Obama," "Women for Obama," and so on. If you added only the next top-20 groups, Obama would have an additional 2 million supporters. This is in stark contrast to John McCain who had 614,000 supporters for his fan page the day of the election and whose next largest fan page was for his wife Cindy with only 1,700 fans. That's 5.1 million (Obama) to less than 1 million (McCain). On MySpace, Obama had 833,161 friends to McCain's 217,811, and this type of disparity held true on Twitter where Obama attracted 113,000 followers to McCain's 4,650.[2]

Obama Was Made for YouTube

Looking to YouTube, the disparity was even greater closer to the election. The BarackObamadotcom YouTube channel had over 20 million views, whereas the johnmccaindotcom channel had just over 2 million views.[3] A year and a half prior to the election, a more attractive than talented girl released the "I have a crush on Barack Obama video." This was prior to "Obamamania" sweeping the country; in fact, it was items like this that helped fuel it. This video was viewed

11.5 million times in the months leading up to the election.[4] In McCain's defense, his voting base skewed older, and they didn't use these types of tools so prevalently at the time, which meant a huge advantage for Obama. Obama used social media to his advantage in both the Democratic and National race to become the president of the United States.

This leveraging of peer-to-peer communication helped mitigate the violent swings that can be caused by traditional media and is one significant reason why Obama was able to overcome some controversial issues (e.g., Reverend Jeremiah Wright, William Ayers) during his campaign for the oval office.

"No one knows the impact of quasi-permanency on the Web yet, but it surely has changed the political world," said Allan Louden, a professor who teaches a course on digital politics at Wake Forest University. "The role of gatekeepers and archivists have been dispersed to everyone with Internet access."[5]

Obama Sings in the Shower—Behind-the-Scenes Content

Obama's team was also creative by providing their own original footage of events that the networks would have died to have—behind the scene moments. They were able to splice these together with decent, yet not high-end, production quality. Even if they had the money, you wouldn't necessarily want top-level editing because that destroys the authenticity of the organic ambiance you are attempting to create and, more important, increased the lag time to get the content in the hands of the socialmediorati (term for active social media users). Viewers are interested in timely information that they can relate to—spending time and money on high-end production can often create distance between candidate and viewer. Viewers are interested in how a person acts when the lights of Hollywood aren't on—how does the candidate interact with his family and those closest to him on a day-by-day basis.

Said social media user Lance Muller of Decatur, Georgia, "I have been an Obama friend since his speech at the 2004 Democratic

Convention. In social media, he actually virtually "pokes" me and sends memos and stuff. I don't know if it is really him, but it makes you feel more in touch with the process. His team is smart in utilizing social networks to reach people like me so that I feel connected personally."[6]

Knowing that social media users rely on the general freedom afforded by the Web, the Obama camp was smart in appealing to their base by introducing a Chief Technology Offer (CTO) position to the President's cabinet; which was dependent on an Obama victory. The main role of the CTO is to "ensure that our government and all its agencies have the right infrastructure, policies, and services for the twenty-first century."[7]

As we will discuss throughout this book, advertisers need to become providers of content. Obama's campaign did just that when they placed ads pushing an early voting message in EA games, most prominently in a racing game called "Burnout Paradise." These games are socially interactive, with kids being able to compete with each other around the globe. Obama's objective for this particular campaign targeted players in 10 battleground states. The key again to this form of advertising is that it benefits the player of the game, the game appears more real-time with seamless and wireless updates to allow for such real-time product placement—in this case the product placement was Obama with the specific message of early voting.

When you look at total views for Obama via YouTube, they accounted for 110 million views. This was estimated at 14.5 million hours of viewing on YouTube, according to Democratic political consultant Joe Trippi. He estimated that amount of time would have cost $47 million to purchase in commercial time.[8]

"If not for the Internet, Barack Obama would not be president or even the democratic nominee," claimed Arianna Huffington of the liberal Huffington Post web site.[9] Overall blog mentions of "Obama" and "McCain" varied greatly during the election (and we can't delineate positive versus negative posts), close to 500 million blog postings mentioned Obama since the beginning of the conventions. During the same time period, only about 150 million blog posts mentioned McCain.[10]

Obama's almost micropayment style approach to fund raising allowed him to outspend McCain nearly three-to-one, which was a testament to the capabilities of social media. By engaging constituents directly, they were able to raise an incredible $660 million in campaign contributions.[11]

Close to 65 percent of the American population voted in the 2008 election, the highest turnout since the election of 1908.[12] These results are telling; a Democrat had not won Virginia and Indiana since then either. Obama captured both.

Support came from everywhere for Obama during his historic and meteoric political run. Some help came from unexpected places. The famous Budweiser "Whassup" commercials, which debuted in 1999, immediately helped sell millions of Bud Lights. The ad became a part of our pop culture following its exposure during the 2000 Super Bowl. Could this same whassup idea be resurrected to help Obama's cause for change? You bet.

The parody used the same characters from the original spots and opens in the exact same fashion, but instead of the character comfortably relaxed on the couch, he is sitting on a foldout chair in a boxed-up apartment as a subtle hint at the housing crisis that was sweeping the country in 2008.

From there, the spoof took off with a series of whassup conversations in conference call fashion. The characters range from one friend stationed in Iraq, another fighting a hurricane, someone looking for help to pay for pain medication because of a broken arm, and the star of the original commercials, "Dookie," steals the show again as he contemplates hanging himself after seeing his entire stock portfolio go essentially down to zero. Dookie being overweight pulls the entire ceiling fan down, hence it still keeps its original light tone while at the same time connects with the audience and seeds a strong message. At the end of the video one of the characters asks again, "Whassup?" And the main character replies, "Change. Change, that's whassup," from his boxed-up apartment as he watches TV images of Senator Obama and his wife.

"It's a great juxtaposition of the original ads. It shows how the lives of these characters have dramatically changed in the past eight years—going from carefree and relaxed beer buddies to being confronted by a shift in global dynamics, an economic collapse, and all in all an unbelievable amount of personal challenge and difficulty. Being able to identify with the characters is what makes this so strong, and they never once say or state Obama's name, rather it's a subtle glimpse of Barack and Michelle Obama on the television that the main character is watching at the end the spot with a huge smile on this face. The short video ending with the word 'True' just like in the 1999 commercials that were followed by the word 'Change' was both powerful and brilliant," said author and political campaign expert Brian Reich.[13]

Reich was a key member of the Howard Dean interactive team largely recognized as the originators of many of the political Internet tactics that Obama successfully leveraged.

Charles Stone III, who was the idea man behind the original Budweiser ads, created this satire. The ad was posted on October 24, 2008 on social media site YouTube; a little over a week prior to the election and received over 4.8 million views along with 14,891 user comments. Also 21,746 viewers took the time to rate the video and it received the difficult-to-achieve ultimate 5-star rating.[14]

Stone was paid roughly $37,000 by Anheuser-Busch and Omnicom Group's DDB Chicago for the rights to license the concept for five years. Stone originally had created a "whassup" film that had caught Omnicom's attention. The fact that neither Anheuser-Busch nor their agency owned the rights to the concept is unusual in the advertising business, but in this instance, it allowed Stone to make his popular and effective parody. Stone appears in both the original and satire ads with his buddies—who also happen to be African American. Stone felt that he could use the same concept to "make a difference" for a politician he believes in.[15]

In this instance, the brand is Obama. The Obama camp could have asked Stone to remove the video out of concern that the "hanging scene" and "soldier in Iraq" may have pushed the line too far. A traditional brand would have stopped this and diluted its viral power. Obama did not do this; instead, he allowed someone (Stone) outside of his camp to take ownership of the brand and promote it. As a result, he exposed his message to 4.8 million people right before the election without spending one penny or lifting one finger. That is the power of social media for brands.

However, it's important also not to underestimate the potential bumps in the road when your supporters are a little too aggressive with your brand. This was the case with another video that was in support of Obama. This one was aptly named "Politics as Usual" and was produced by famous hip-hop artist Ludacris. One of the lines was "Obama would paint the White House black." This was tame in comparison to dismissing Hillary Clinton as a potential vice presidential running mate—"that bitch is irrelevant." Attacking the Republicans, Ludacris stated that John McCain should only be able to sit in the "big chair" if he is paralyzed. This rap video received over a million views on YouTube.[16]

It was a tough spot for Obama to be in because he still wanted the support of the influential hip-hop community, but also needed to avoid the controversy that these lyrics stirred. He did the right thing and quickly publicly denounced it, calling the music video "outrageously offensive." "While Ludacris is a talented individual, he should be ashamed of these lyrics," Obama campaign spokesman Bill Burton said in an e-mail statement.

"Of course, Obama and his people have to condemn the rap, because it does say some vulgar things. If you're running for president, you're supposed to be an upstanding individual," said John McWhorter author of *All About the Beat: Why Hip-Hop Can't Save Black America*.[17] Many companies and politicians make the mistake of stopping there, but Obama went the extra mile to have a private meeting with the rap star. Rapper Ludacris said Barack Obama disapproved of the song he wrote because it insulted his rivals.

"The song was my artistic expression and was meant to get people who weren't involved in the political process involved. Being as though it was the first mix tape to reach the United States government, it was a bit overwhelming," said Ludacris. He indicated that when he met with Obama they didn't just discuss the song. "What myself and the president spoke about is confidential, but I took it upon myself to not speak about the song."[18] By acting quickly and decisively, Obama was able to turn a negative into a positive, for he kept the support of Ludacris' fan base while distancing himself from the controversial content.

Can Google Predict the Next President or Flu Outbreak?

In the early part of this century, Yahoo started to leverage the search data that was flowing into its data centers. At the time, Yahoo was the world's preeminent search engine. They were noticing that they could predict some pop-culture trends often six weeks in advance. They actually leveraged this data for one of their biggest advertising clients at the time, Pepsi-Cola. They identified through their "buzz index" that searches for an up-and-coming pop star by the name of Britney Spears were indexing "off the charts" and rising rapidly. As a perk to their important client, Yahoo disclosed this information, and Pepsi seized the opportunity. With little investment, Pepsi was able to sign Spears to a relatively cheap endorsement contract a few months before she became one of the music industry's biggest and brightest stars.

Fast forward to the present. Because of the transparency that social media demands, search engines don't hold this data hostage anymore. Much of the search data is open for public consumption. While the data is in aggregate (meaning privacy policies are upheld since you can't identify an individual) and the data isn't absolute (meaning there are indexes rather than the actual number of searches—otherwise Wall Street analysts could extrapolate data to predict quarterly financial performance for the search engines) it is very helpful for myriad items.

Is the Flu a Virus or Just Simply Viral?

It appears that people make the habit of entering phrases like "flu symptoms" or "flu remedies" into search engines prior to actually going in for a doctor's visit. When you multiply this across millions of searches around the globe, you have something like a neighborhood watch for fast-spreading flu outbreaks.

"Google flu trends" is a service provided by the company's philan-thropic arm (Google.org), released to do just exactly that. Historically, the Center for Disease Control (CDC) based in Atlanta, Georgia, was the only source for tracking spikes in viruses like the flu. Comparing the CDC data to Google's data showed that Google's insight was roughly two weeks ahead of the CDC. The CDC data is inherently slower as a result of its dependence on data being supplied and ana-lyzed from thousands of sources (e.g., doctors, labs, health insurance).

This is powerful stuff that could stifle the spread of disease and ulti-mately save lives. Google is able to combine flu search data with their robust mapping tools to quickly showcase where the disease is spread-ing across the world. The potential doesn't stop at influenza, but can be used for all forms of disease and outbreak. The CDC data and other data could also be combined with the search data to make it even stronger. "Most forecasting is basically trend extrapolation," said Hal Varian, Google's chief economist. "This works remarkably well, but tends to miss turning points, times when the data changes direction. Our hope is that Google data might help with this problem."[19] The key is that the data has always existed and in some instances was being used (e.g., Pepsi and Britney Spears), but socialnomics has been a main driver behind it being shared for such beneficial causes.

In 2009, Prabhakar Raghavan, the head of Yahoo Labs said search data could be valuable for forecasters and scientists, but privacy con-cerns had generally stopped Yahoo Labs from sharing it with outside academics. "I think we are just scratching the surface of what's possi-ble with collective intelligence,"[20] said Thomas W. Malone, a profes-sor at the Sloan School of Management at MIT. For business and politics it is very intriguing: Do more people search: "cheap travel" or "travel"? "Coke" or "Pepsi"? "Obama" or "McCain"?

This last one was particularly intriguing. Could search data help predict the next president of the United States?

Indiana Goes Google Gaga for Obama

We compared U.S. search trends in April for the terms "Clinton," "McCain," and "Obama." Total searches for Obama far exceeded those of Clinton. For every Clinton search, there were 1.60 Obama searches. Yet, for every Clinton search, there were only .48 McCain searches.[21]

This makes sense, because the Democrats were in a heated primary. What's interesting is that Obama had so many more searches than Clinton. Keep in mind that Clinton is artificially inflated by the fact that it contains searches having nothing to do with Hillary (e.g., people looking for Bill, Clinton Township). Obama is a unique term, so it has less statistical noise. Also, the data doesn't factor in searches done for "Barack." So, Obama's 1.60:1 ratio was most likely even higher than the numbers indicated.

Other Google Insights data pointed out that in April of 2008 searches for Obama in the state of Indiana greatly exceeded those of Clinton. It would've been easy to predict that Obama was closing the gap on Hillary in that state. After all, if the voters had already decided to vote for Hillary, there wouldn't be a need to search for information on Obama. Obama was supposed to lose handily in Indiana; but just as the data predicted, he closed the gap, narrowly lost the state, but was well on his way to achieving the nomination afterward.

Canada Cared the Most about the Next U.S. President

Google Insights data also gave strong indications that Obama would defeat John McCain in the presidential election. Thirty days prior to the election, Obama searches outperformed McCain almost 3:1 even though McCain had gained 11 percent in search volume over the same time period. Predictably, U.S. allies seem the most interested in the election (Canada, United Kingdom, etc.) judging by their search behavior. Global searches indexed even higher for Obama over McCain by a 4:1 ratio, indicating that the world was also ready for a change. In the United States, not surprisingly, most searches for Obama and McCain came from those living in Washington, DC, and the same held true for college towns, Austin, Texas, and Raleigh, North Carolina, which indexed within the top 10 primarily due to the youthful supporters being so involved in this election.[22]

McCain and Obama each tried to build up their respective *brands* in the eyes of voters. They used search data to answer questions such as: Is it better to print "Obama" or "Barack" on promotional posters. There were 3.5 more searches done on "Obama" than "Barack."[23] Pretty helpful information.

Just like in the political race, search data can also be used in the world of business to help guide companies in making strategic decisions. Should Coke use the term "soda pop" or "soda" to describe the products on its web site? What regions in the world search for "Coke" more than "Pepsi"? In future elections, such search data will be used more and more by all constituents.

Fireside Chats and Presidential Texts

In a text message sent to supporters on the eve of the election, Obama reaffirmed that they would be part of the presidency, "We have a lot of work to do to get our country back on track, and I'll be in touch soon about what comes next."

Obama was smart in not abandoning social media once he took over as the president. He realized that the people who elected him to office also wanted to stay connected, and he also knows this will be his key to success as president. Just as users are willing to take ownership of brands when given the chance, if they understand it is their government and not Obama's, then there really is a true chance for change. Change comes from within, not externally.

Social media allows for this two-way conversation. The U.S. president, for the first time, can cultivate grassroots communities directly where people discover, create, and share information online. Obama has pledged to involve Americans in his decision making, by giving them five days to comment online on any nonemergency legislation before he signs it.

To help with this conversation, Obama has resurrected the principals of FDR's fireside radio chats; only this time, these chats will be on YouTube or another online video format, which allows for commentary, posts, rebuttals, and ongoing dialog. His cabinet members are also committed to having their own chats as well. The goal is to make the political process more transparent and give an identity to the White House. This is exactly the same strategy that good brands employ; transparency and having people connect and identify with the brand because the brand helps define them. Good companies put customers' needs first and foremost.

Whether you're a Republican, Democrat, Independent, or member of the Bull Moose Party, you can't deny the power of real-world community relations combined with the reach and engagement of online social communities and networks to change politics as usual. It's important to note that this isn't about using the latest "shiny new toy" out there. The key resides in the ability to identify and internalize issues that help precipitate change. Action earns support, not merely words.

As addressed in our preventative and braggadocian behavior sections of this book, it is important for the president to be transparent by showing the behind-the-scenes inner workings of the White House without sacrificing national security. It is irrelevant whether you like the transparent demands of social media or don't like them; the fact is that society has drastically changed as a result of social media—this isn't just a nice perk for the presidency to use, it is something the public now demands.

It's an opportunity for government to meet demands by using new and influential channels to address voters' needs and win people over, one citizen at a time.

The office of the president will never be able to satisfy everyone, but if social media is utilized correctly, it will supply the ideas, insights, support, concerns, and satisfaction of the American public. It allows for a government to be more in tune with the country and to truly run as a democracy by stripping away the politics and getting to the core of what matters. Sometimes the best advisors are those who voted against the elect in the first place. Mr. Obama offers this message to his supporters during his closing arguments at a Democratic campaign rally in Canton, Ohio:

I ask you to believe—not just in my ability to bring about change, but in yours. I know this change is possible ... because in this campaign, I have had the privilege to witness what is best in America. The story of the campaign and this historic moment has been your story. It is about the great things we can do when we come together around a common purpose. The story of bringing this country together as a healed and united nation will be led by President-Elect Obama, but written by you. The millions of you who built this campaign from the ground up, and echoed your call for the change you wanted to see implemented by the Obama Administration—this process of setting up that new government is about you.[24]

In 2008, the Gartner Group hypothesized that social media would complement and even replace some functions of the government. For some people, this may seem laughable, but isn't that what the U.S. government is supposed to be about—a government of the people, for the people, and by the people? This will become even more prevalent with Obama's successor whether they are Republican, Democrat, or Independent. As the 2008 presidential campaign's reliance on social media to persuade voters indicates, this will become an integral part of every candidate's campaign in the years to come, particularly considering that this election's online campaigns will be scrutinized more than any before. "There's going to be a lot of analysis of the campaign online this time around," Borrell's VP of Research Kip Cassino told ClickZ News. "This is absolutely a groundbreaking election for digital marketing and the candidates, and it's not just the money involved. It's the techniques that were developed and the knowledge that was gained."[25]

Is the White House More BlackBerry or Mayberry?

Of course everything isn't all roses for Obama and his pioneering ways. Days after the election, a decision had to be made on whether Obama could keep his BlackBerry, something that he, like many others, had become dependent on in his daily life. In fact, in one White House meeting everyone was asked to put his or her BlackBerry in the middle of the table to ensure that each person was paying attention.

This was something new for Washington, but not for businesses that had already assigned the device's addictive ways an apt nickname—"crackberry."

The reason for the discussion about whether Obama would need to relinquish his BlackBerry did not center on overuse. Rather, it revolved around the fact that his text messaging, tweets, status updates, and e-mails would be a part of public record. When George Bush entered the White House, he had to give up his AOL account (G94B@aol.com) for this exact reason. So, Obama's friendly joshing and trash-talking with his buddies about the latest Bears playoff game would be public record. However, relating back to our discussion on preventative and braggadocian behavior, has Obama been around social media long enough to have established the correct behavior and fail-safes associated with the new world around us?

Perhaps so, which then allows for the use of such devices as a BlackBerry to transform information into an asset. Rick Sanchez of CNN uses Twitter to grow his user base. He raised his CNN program to number three, only behind Fox News *O'Reilly Factor* and MSNBC's *Keith Olbermann's Countdown.* Because of Sanchez's success, viewers' microblog posts are a part of almost every CNN broadcast.

Does a president's transparency become an enormous asset? Can he go from a million followers on Twitter to 100 million? As president of the United States, his public record may be quite different from that of Joe Plumber's, but the reasons for utilizing it are the same—to communicate transparently. People are using these mechanisms as a public record. There are no secrets; we are living in a world of glass houses. That is why Obama may be the first president to keep his BlackBerry or have the first presidential laptop computer. We know the positive impact of these tools, and one of the most powerful people in the world should still have the option to use them.

To Sarah Palin's credit, she seemed to be practicing correct preventative behavior. When her Yahoo e-mail was hacked into, there was not much *dirt* to be found, which is a credit to her because these were supposed to be private conversations; it was a social media forum. San

Francisco Mayor Gavin Newsom agreed that for national politics the Obama campaign used social media to an unprecedented level. "Now I'm more concerned with what it means when we can use this unfiltered conversation with people. How will it help construct public policy?" he asked.[26]

While Obama benefited enormously from the power of social media, there are still his social media detractors. A Facebook group was formed prior to Obama even taking office with several hundred members called "Impeach Barack Obama." Social media has the good, bad, and the ugly for everyone to see. When it comes to politics, isn't that the true beauty of social media? Its power speaks for itself; before social media, Obama would not have even won his own party's nomination, let alone become the 44th president of the United States.

Free Pancakes Anyone?

Starbuck's, Ben & Jerry's, and others gave freebies on Election Day—did it work? Remember the free pancake breakfast you used to get as a kid down at the fire station? Of course it wasn't free, your parents would pay a donation to help out the firefighters, but it seemed like it was free, didn't it? Your parents likely donated more than they would have paid at the local Denny's for a "Grand Slam" breakfast, yet they too felt it was free, probably better than free even.

This is the sense of community that human beings long for, and it is something that isn't lost with social media. In fact, it is part of the reason for social media's meteoric ascendancy in our lives. Face-to-face interaction still can't be beat, but social media does help you feel part of a community. It is even able to help keep an intimate community feel on a national or global level. A good example of this was the 2008 U.S. presidential election.

In year's past, there have been many campaigns that attempted to increase voter turnout (e.g., MTV's Rock the Vote). Few have seemed to work. In 2008, voter turnout was predicted to be strong for many reasons, but as a friendly reminder and incentive, several companies gave away freebies on Election Day. Generally most marketers steer clear of anything political, but in this case, the brand marketers wanted to be a part of a community, and the community in this instance, thanks to social media, was the American community.

Some of the more high-profile giveaways included a chicken sandwich from Chick-fil-A, a tall cup of coffee from Starbucks, a free scoop of ice cream from Ben & Jerry's, and a star-shaped doughnut with "patriotic sprinkles" (i.e., red, white, and blue) from Krispy Kreme. Along with many other factors, these freebies helped drive the highest voter turnout since 1908.[27]

For users to get their freebies they had to show their "I Voted" sticker, but in most cases, they could simply say they voted. (After all, isn't community all about trust?) One entity that doesn't believe in trust was the government; it almost rained on this feel-good parade by highlighting a federal law that stipulates you can't give incentives to encourage people to vote. Fortunately, several companies didn't let this hurdle stop them and were able to work within it.

That is another example of the changes we are seeing with the advent of socialnomics—it's a new way of thinking. In the past, big companies like this would have been *shrinking violets* and would have let their well-paid legal counsel pontificate on doomsday scenarios and suck the enthusiasm out of the marketing and public relations departments until they gave up on the idea.

Today we are seeing less of this, partially due to the intense competition forcing companies to adopt the mantra: *"If we don't do this, someone else will."* Part of this competition is coming from foreign entities that don't have the same legal requirements as U.S. based entities. Most of all, though, we are seeing companies and people within companies with the conviction to drive what they believe is best for the company even if it clashes with the opinion of legal counsel. If companies have confidence in what they are doing, then they will overcome the hurdles that formerly may have blocked them.

Contributing to this, in part, is the flexibility and real-time nature of social media. In the past, if Ben & Jerry's was going to promote a free giveaway via the expensive development of television, radio, and print advertising, then they would have to think twice about the concerns of the law shutting down their good intentions, because it would be quite costly. However, because the primary push for this promotion was by sending an alert to their followers on the Ben & Jerry's Handmade Inc. Facebook fan page, there were few upfront costs, and the action of taking down the promotion was roughly only 20 to 30 minutes of work.

The variable cost of how many people show up for the freebies remains a factor, but it is the fixed costs of print and production of advertising that causes marketers to think twice about a promotion if there is a chance that it would be shut down for legal reasons. Social media helps mitigate these concerns because the upfront costs are so minimal that if a legal issue shuts down the program at the last minute, so be it. Also, social media allows things to be shut down in a few minutes, and for word to travel just as quickly. In this instance, if Ben & Jerry's needed to shut down, they simply inform their 285,000 Facebook fans and let them spread the word virally.

As we will constantly harp on within social media, it's not how cool Ben & Jerry's is, but rather can they give their loyal fans something to pass on that makes *them* (loyal fans) look cool? "I didn't know about the B&J free ice cream giveaway until my friend Stephen in Texas pushed it my way on Facebook. It was good to know he was thinking about me, and I felt like I owed him a scoop of ice cream," said Kim (Nashville, Tennessee).[28] During the promotion Ben & Jerry's added over 100,000 fans to their Facebook fan page resulting in a total of 385,000 fans.[29]

Starbucks promoted their coffee giveaway almost exclusively via social media mechanisms. They ran only one ad on *SNL;* which was primarily viral during the time because of the success of the Tina Fey-Sarah Palin spoofs (more than 50 percent of the views were within social media). They also ran 30 TV spots on Hulu and displayed placements on Facebook. The spots took advantage of the well-known Starbuck's recycled paper brown coffee sleeve to animate and script a quick message helping to convey two salient points—we care about the environment and we care about the country. The message was "What if we cared so much every day about these things?" In a rare instance, it covered off branding (what Starbucks stands for) and also gave a call to action (come to our store). It is estimated that Starbuck's spent less than $400,000 for this promotion, which Oprah quickly paid back by giving it some major coverage on her show as did every other media outlet (including this book). On YouTube alone the promotion received 386,000 views.

One measure that tracks this type of viral buzz (amount people that are talking or writing about your brand) indicated that Starbucks' buzz increased +26 percent as a result of this effort.[30] While Starbuck's would not disclose how much coffee was given away, in some stores it was plenty: one Chicago franchise handed out 300 steaming cups of Java and goodwill.[31] Facebook users also started downloading the application *"Which Drink Is Meant for You"* resulting in almost 100,000 active monthly users, driving Starbuck's fan page to nearly 200,000 fans.[32] In order for companies to truly benefit from social media, they have to become part of the community. Is your company serving up fresh pancakes or stale messaging?

Social Media Creates and also Solves Long Voting Lines

To help assuage concerns about long lines due to record voter turnout a Twitter Vote Report was established. Voters who were at the poles could use the microblogging tool to help supply real-time data on polling conditions. These problem messages or alerts were aggregated and applied to a Google Mapping tool so that people could see any voting issues in their area in the hopes of avoiding crowds and hassle. It was very simple to send in reports using your mobile device:

#wait:90 = Wait time is 90 minutes

#machine:30 = Wait time is 30 minutes due to machine issues

Users who didn't use Twitter could also send text messages to #voterreport, to 66, or call an automated hotline. Hashtangs or # are very convenient when using microblogging tools or text messaging, as they allow items to be easily tagged and categorized—which has been a dramatic part of the social media revolution. Convenient items like this contributed to the 2008 elections having the highest voter turnout in 100 years.[33] Higher voter turnout is one positive influence that social media has on society.

Online Voting—The Future Is Now

If the political use of social media accelerates in the future, what new and exciting tactics can we expect? One thing that is surely inevitable is the introduction of online voting. Having the capability to easily cast votes via online mechanisms makes too much sense for it not to become a reality. For those who have always screamed that online voting is less secure than offline voting, you clearly do not understand the current offline process to obtain an absentee ballot. Let me explain.

For the 2008 presidential election, for the state of Florida, which one could argue should have the tightest system after the difficulties the state experienced in the 2000 election, the offline security was less than tight. For example, prospective voters were required to know (1) birth date and (2) address number, not the entire address, just the mailbox number! If you had these two relatively easy-to-access pieces of information, the state of Florida was happy to send you an absentee ballot to any address that you specified.

If you were a legitimate absentee voter and dutifully filled out your form, you proceeded to drop it in the mail. The outside of the envelope boldly proclaims ABSENTEE BALLOT, and it also has your authorized signature on the outside of it! Anywhere along the way this ballot could be conveniently lost or stolen by numerous people. That doesn't sound nearly as secure as an online process that has point-to-point encryption with only those two points having the proper access key

This is analogous to when the Internet was first introduced to the masses as a place of commerce, aptly named e-commerce. It's hard to believe now, but at the time people were afraid to give out their credit card numbers online because of the false belief it was unsafe to do so. Yet, these same people had no problem giving it to some random clerk along with their signature at the local convenience store. For now, let's assume that great minds are able to solve the major security holes in online voting (they will). Imagine the tremendous increase in voter participation when this occurs! In a SodaHead study, 79 percent of the respondents said they wouldn't wait an hour to vote during the 2008 presidential election.[34]

People can argue that not everyone has a computer or mobile device that can access the Web. While this is true, there are more people who have the ability to access the Web than have voting machines in their houses. Those who don't have access to the Web can go to their local library or voting station just as they have in the past. The cost savings associated with no longer dealing with paper, staffing, parking, administration, voting machines, police protection, and so on would be significant. The increase in productivity would also be mind-boggling.

Assuming the U.S. population is approximately 310 million, and according to the latest U.S. census bureau data, 68 percent are of voting age, this equates to 210 million possible voters.[35] If the average hourly wage (factoring in white collar) is close to $16, and keeping in mind that drive time along with the physical act of voting takes an average of two hours, the summation is starting. This is $6.7 billion in lost productivity (210 million x $16 per hour x 2 hours)! All that could be saved by a few simple clicks online.

The harder decisions aren't necessarily based on if we introduce online voting or not, but rather how it will function when it is introduced. There are several social behavioral pieces to keep in mind. Is early voting online a capability? It makes sense. Because counting is automatic are the early voting results disclosed to the public so that everyone can see how the race is projecting? If someone has already cast his or her vote is that person allowed to go back and change it anytime before the election? In other words, how social would the government allow online voting to become? It would make sense to make it very social. For example—early voters could click on a radio button or have a form field for the main reason they selected or didn't select a certain candidate. Imagine, candidates could then address the concerns of the voting public during the election process itself. Sounds democratic to me.

Even the Army Is Sharing Information

In an effort to relate with their desired target audience of 17- to 24-year-olds, the Army launched a tool called "Straight from Iraq." It was designed to allow potential recruits to get a better sense of what war is like from the people who know best. This is a long way from the days in Vietnam where television coverage was carefully screened. "Straight from Iraq" was historic because it was the first time that candidates could ask direct questions of soldiers in combat.

"The goal is to provide those considering the Army—along with parents and others who influence their decisions—with verifiable information about what being a soldier is really like, what combat is really like," said Lt. Gen. Benjamin C. Freakley, at the time commanding general of the Army Accessions Command in Fort Monroe, Va., which is overseeing recruitment.[36]

"The campaign was successful in conveying the benefits of 'Army strong'—the physical, emotional, and mental benefits," said Ed Walters, chief marketing officer for the Army at the Pentagon.

"We wanted to more clearly articulate that," he added, through efforts like sharing with civilians the video clips of "real soldiers' stories."[37]

As we point out throughout the book, these types of open, social media conversations are much more effective than a unilateral communication to your audience. The best part too is that they are much more cost effective. In this example, while the Army couldn't disclose exact figures, it easily exceeded its recruiting goals for 2006 to 2008.[38]

For cost effectiveness comparison, the Army spent roughly $170 million per year on such high-profile items as NASCAR sponsorships and Rodeos. I'm sure it's fun for the Army's Director of Marketing to watch his NASCAR automobile go around the track every Sunday, but how effective is this, and how accurately can you track such a thing? The average sponsorship cost for a NASCAR is in the $15 to $20 million range. In comparison, the social media campaign costs between $200,000 and $300,000.

Chapter Four Key Points

1. Open, two-way conversations are much more effective than unilateral communications to your audience, for politics and business. Social media enables these two-way conversations. Utilizing free social media tools and placements is more timely and cost effective than traditional advertising.

2. By engaging voters, social media has had a positive impact on voter turnout (the highest since 1908 and the highest youth participation).

3. The adoption of online voting in the future could save an estimated $6.7 billion in lost productivity (U.S. presidential election).

4. We are just scratching the surface of what's possible with collective intelligence in terms of being able to predict and control influenza outbreaks, predicting the United Kingdom's next Prime Minister, and so forth.

5. Fortune 500 companies should learn from Obama's faith in social media and allowance of the public to take ownership of his brand and grow it to unexpected level of success.

6. Just like businesses, politicians and governments need to keep up with advancements in social media, otherwise they will be left behind. Successfully leveraging social media in politics pays big dividends—we need only look at Obama's 2008 victory. *Obama would not be president without the Internet.*

Chapter Five

I Care More about What My Neighbor Thinks than What Google Thinks

Socialommerce is on us. What is socialommerce exactly? It is a term that encompasses the transactional, search, and marketing components of social media. Socialommerce harnesses the simple idea that people value the opinion of other people. Nielsen reports 78 percent of people trust their peers' opinions.[1] This is neither a new concept, nor new to the Web (e.g., epinions.com, complaints.com, angieslist.com).

What is new is that social networks make it so much easier to disseminate information. As the success of social media proves, people like disseminating information. This explains the popularity of Twitter and other microblogging tools. These tools/products enable users to inform their friends what they are doing every minute of the day (I'm having an ice cream cone, check out this great article, listening to keynote speaker, etc.). Microblogging's popularity was originally relegated to teens, but then it quickly gained popularity with adults and businesses. It also played an important role in the 2008 presidential election.

> Social media is creating something that I think eventually is going to be very healthy for our economy, and that is institutional brand integrity.
> —John Gerzema, Chief Insights Officer, Young & Rubicam[2]

The most popular feature of Facebook and LinkedIn is status updates. Status updates enable users to continuously brag, boast, inform, and vent to everyone in their network. This simple tool allows users to easily stay connected with their network. As a result, 100 billion stories—updates per day are processed through Facebook's News Feed servers—100 billion! Let's take a look at a couple examples of Socialommerce in Action.

Buying the Right Baby Seat

Steve and his wife just had their first child. With this addition, they are in the market for a lightweight, but safe, baby seat for their car. Steve doesn't know the first thing about baby seats and is dreading the hours of researching and then searching on the Internet to find the appropriate one. Steve, like many fathers, is also fearful that he may, despite all of his diligent research, still make a mistake. Making sure you provide the appropriate safety for your child can be stressful and at times overwhelming. The good news is that the majority of these purchase challenges, concerns and unwanted stress will become things of the past with social media. Here's why.

On a search engine if you typed "buying a baby seat" you are likely to receive a series of irrelevant search results and a bevy of sponsored ads. Not all of the search results are unrelated. Some will prove fruitful, but it may take some time-intensive trial and error. Yet, as socialommerce becomes more and more mainstream, when Steve performs a search on his favorite social network instead of a search engine and types this same query—"buying a baby seat"—he will discover the following:

- 23 of Steve's 181 friends have purchased a baby seat in the last two years.
- 14 purchased the same make and model.
- The average price for the most popular model $124.99 (10 of the 14 purchased online).
- 3 are looking to sell their used baby seats because their children have outgrown them.
- 7 different online videos showcasing this seat have been

bookmarked—tagged by people in this network.

- 4 different reviews and articles have been bookmarked—tagged by his network.
- 11 of the 14 have posted reviews on the baby seat—two of which are video reviews.

Steve respects the opinions of the 14 people who purchased the same seat, so he clicks to find out more, and gets the following information:

> We have three kids and have used this same baby seat model for all of them. My sister used Cheekie Brand's baby seat and it was clunky, awkward, and heavy. When she saw mine, she immediately went out and got two for her kids. I highly recommend these seats!
> —Jill Higgins

Steve can now confidently purchase the baby seat without the usual research, stress, and time required if he were starting his search from scratch. Once Steve starts to use the seat, he takes on a different roll within the same social media conversation; he is actively using the product and can provide his own insight into features and benefits that the seat provides. Steve may notice that it's too easy for his child to undo one of the seat straps. Compelled, he may point this out to his network via a quick video example that may be relevant to his social network of friends. This then presents an opportunity for product improvement on which the manufacturer can act.

If the manufacturer's marketing team is listening and watching, then they will be able to quickly share this with the design and production team and hopefully get a quick resolution/improvement for future buyers. This is not only a benefit for the manufacturer, but a benefit to society as well, because future children will be much safer based on the quick advancements.

Correspondingly, just like his friends before him, if Steve finds features he really enjoys about the baby seat he will feel compelled to write about them, since his friends with a similar purchase decision will benefit from his experience. When I worked at EarthLink, one of the key findings we found when working on referral incentives was that the main reason people recommended EarthLink was not for the incentive, but that they liked being viewed as the subject matter expert within their social graph. The same holds true in social media.

> The popular belief that people only take the time to post something when they want to vent or discuss a bad experience is simply not true; at least in our experience. The majority of our over 20 million reviews and opinions we have received on TripAdvisor are positive ones. People are simply compelled to give back to a community that has given to them.
> —Steve Kaufer, CEO of TripAdvisor

Minivan or Hybrid?

Steve and his wife then eventually go on to have their third child. With this addition, his two sedans won't cut it anymore, so he's in the market for a bigger vehicle. Having vowed to himself and his friends that he'd never own a minivan, he's in the market for an SUV or a crossover vehicle.

Steve is dreading the hours of searching on the Internet to find a vehicle that suits his needs. He's dreading even more having to leave work early to visit the car dealerships to test-drive his selected vehicles and then begin the haggling process. Steve is also fearful that he may make a mistake even after all of his diligent research.

Steve performs a search on his favorite social network—he types in "buying a car." Rather than receiving a bunch of irrelevant ads for car trader sites he discovers the following:

- 23 of Jim's friends have purchased a car in the last year.
- 16 of his friends are married with two or more children.
- 14 purchased an SUV or crossover.
- 9 purchased the same vehicle.

Steve respects the opinions of the nine people who purchased the same vehicle, so he clicks to find out more, and gets the following information: "I test-drove Crossover X and Crossover Y. Crossover Y was the much better feel, and it was easier to get into the backseat. Couple that with the fact that it gets three more mph to the gallon, and it was a no-brainer."

To further illustrate the importance of virulence today, a study conducted by online-market-research firm Marketing Evolution on marketing campaigns from Adidas and video-game publisher Electronic Arts within MySpace found that 70 percent of the return on investment was the result of one consumer passing it onto another virally. Socialommerce is a referral program on steroids.

Blowing an IRS Refund

Karen (age 48) just received her IRS refund check for $170. She feels like treating herself by buying something, but doesn't have anything particular in mind. Karen quickly taps into her social network to see what other people she respects (friends/peers) are buying and whether they like or dislike their choices.

Within five minutes, she decides to purchase an iPod Nano because her friend Sally bought one and she loves it. The fact that Sally has one and likes it assuaged Karen's fear of technology because Sally is even more of a technical neophyte than Karen. Knowing this about Sally drove 95 percent of Karen's decision process within minutes. This intimate knowledge of people within your social network is key, and is one main reason of why reviews via social media have gone to the "next level" compared to other online reviews in the past.

The big social networks (Facebook, LinkedIn, hi5, etc.) will eventually dominate this portion of socialommerce. Sites like ThisNext, Kaboodle, and WishPot, helped push the adoption of this market opportunity by enabling buyers to quickly share their purchases and reviews with friends. These sites were designed for people to go to for ideas about what products and services they should be purchasing and using.

Bon Voyage Online Travel Agents?

Suzy (age 34) has set aside a budget of $1,400 to take a trip this year with her husband. The only thing she knows at this point: destination, South America. In the past, she would've performed a search on Google, which would have taken her to some helpful online travel agent sites (e.g., Travelzoo, TripAdvisor, GoAhead Tours, Lonely Planet, Orbitz, Priceline, Travelocity). She probably would've narrowed down her choices after hours of research. From there, she would then begin the arduous task of finding the best deal for her flight, hotel, and so on.

As a result of social media, this process becomes much simpler for Suzy. She simply goes to her social network of choice and searches for "South American Vacations." The results pop up: five of her friends have traveled to South America in the last year. Conveniently listed are their itineraries, hotels, and resorts, as well as prices and recommendations.

Suzy sees two of her friends both took a trip to Chile through GoAhead Tours and rated it highly. It's within her budget, and the same package is available. She quickly snatches it up before it's sold out. She saved hours of painstaking research and the fees of a travel agent.

If she only has 10 minutes before going to pick up the kids at day care, is her time better served scrolling through 400 reviews by people she doesn't know on a travel review site (some which will be spam from the competing hotels) or is she better served looking at the recommendations from her friends? The time is much better spent with her friends' experience and recommendations. Socialommerce gave her peace of mind and the anticipation of an enjoyable adventure.

Listed alongside the qualitative reviews are certain data points for each friend: price, travel supplier, places recommended, day excursions, and so on.

We could continue with other examples, like trying to figure out what the trendiest online video game is for Christmas. This has several challenges, the first is trying to figure out what the *it* game is. The second is to determine if it is age appropriate for your child (e.g., sex, violence). Third, if it is the *it* game, the task of obtaining the game will be a challenge. Fortunately, social media lessens many of these worries because some of your early-adopter friends can show the way by providing insight into their purchase history and experiences. If a friend you trust bought the game for her child, that would be more insightful than trying to decipher the confusing game ratings for graphic and sexual content to determine if the product is age appropriate for your own child.

Social media has a much easier time tracking when the purchase is made online. It enables users to know where goods or services were purchased—which in turn may be a good indication that the item is in stock. This is done using cookie-based tracking that follows the user (if they opt in) as they traverse and transact on the Web. A cookie is a term used to describe a tiny piece of code that is placed in your Web browser.

What does this mean for brand marketing? Well, it means that companies and marketers better start spending more time listening to their customers and less time spending countless hours creating the next award-winning, but-no-customer-getting, 30-second television commercial. Consumers are taking ownership of brands, and their referral power is priceless.

Just as important as listening to the customer is acting on the information received. This entails all parts of the organization working more harmoniously than ever before—the speed of social media demands it. These certainly aren't new constructs, but in the age of Web 2.0, your brand will experience a quick death if these constructs aren't adhered to. The days of traditional brand marketing aren't necessarily dead; they're just taking on new forms.

Socialommerce increases efficiency by saving time as it eliminates multiple individual redundancies (MIR). This is obviously a tremendous benefit to the user and mission critical for businesses to understand that this impacts almost everything they do from marketing to operations to manufacturing. As people increasing look to their social networks for advice and recommendations, marketers need to make certain they are part of the consideration set. In order to accomplish this, companies need to create great products and services rather than rely on a fancy advertising campaign to bail them out. When a transaction occurs, marketers need to encourage or give incentives for users to complete product and service reviews albeit good, bad, or indifferent. Companies able to encourage this information sharing from their consumers via both online and offline means, help water the seeds of viral success in social media. Money to water the seeds will come from traditional advertising budgets (television, outdoor, radio) and will go directly into the consumers' pockets. This is another reason why consumers will take more ownership of the brands they associate with, and it makes the traditional referral model look like a dollhouse alongside the Taj Mahal.

Ken Robbins, Founder of Digital Agency Response Mine Interactive sums up the challenges and opportunities that individuals and companies face with social media:

> Social media has evolved from a mere post it-answer it model (bulletin boards and blogs) to instantaneous publish-subscribe models (i.e., Twitter and Facebook updates). Combined with the portable surfing of today's phones, this pub-submodel has both fantastic and dire implications for businesses. It's fantastic from the standpoint that one can not only stand in front of a refrigerator in a store and check out reviews of that model, the consumer can Twitter his network to get advice on all models, this brand and this store instantaneously. If the product and store have good reputations, buying hesitancy is removed and the purchase takes place. The dire side of this is that if the price, the model, or the store has poor reputations, the transaction will definitely not take place. We are moving to a world with total retail and product performance transparency for the consumer. The market will be much less tolerant of poor service and poor products and high margins with this social communications infrastructure.[3]

Many may take umbrage with two points/assumptions being made. One could make a good argument that people aren't going to want to share their purchase decisions. This is true; some will not. Others will share only certain purchase decisions and price points, while still others will share everything and anything. However, from an online buying perspective, the technology for this to occur is there, and as we have seen from the transparency of other social media usage, it's only a matter of time that purchases will be pushed to everyone who is willing.

The other piece that people will be concerned about is that buyers will be incented to write a review. It's possible that a true tangible incentive may not be necessary, but what is certain is that more effort and marketing dollars will be used to implore customers to write a review of their product. This incentive model isn't anything new; when a hotel or airline asks you to fill out a suggestion card, it is usually with the "hook" of potentially winning a sweepstakes or free meal.

The hope is that incentives aren't necessary, but even if they are, that doesn't mean that the person will write a good review. This type of transparent review may not be for everyone, as some people like to remain anonymous, but that brings up another key point: All reviews don't necessarily need to be public to everyone—some may only feel comfortable posting reviews to their own network, which is better than we are today, where that "shy" person isn't posting an reviews or feedback.

All of this is a lot to digest for Generation X and beyond, but it's somewhat of a way of life for the Generations born after 1980, as they have grown up in a transparent world.

We can see a dramatic shift in that 92 percent of consumers now cite word-of-mouth as the best source for product and brand information, up from 67% in 1977.[4] That is one reason why in this book we say we've moved from word-of-mouth to world-of-mouth marketing.

Looking to Friends for Medical Advice

Other major societal benefits from social media will be made in the health care arena. 2008 survey results from online advertising agency iCrossing showed that 34 percent of Americans turn to social media for health research. While substantial, we are certain these numbers are even higher today. Twenty percent of the online health searchers went to *Wikipedia* for information. Other social networks were also used and the average age of people using social media for health related questions was 37 versus the average overall age for patients searching for health information being 44.[5] It is not surprising that it is younger, but it does again show that social media users aren't all teenagers; it will be mainstream sooner than people expect. When health consumers turn to social media they are in a decision-mode process. Needs range from finding out costs for certain operations or medical devices to the reputation of a certain provider or doctor.

When engaged in face-to-face or phone conversation, it can be awkward or even rude to discuss medical conditions. Social media eliminates this awkwardness. A simple post like "Has anyone ever had their appendix removed? I've had a sharp pain in my right side for the last day. Let me know." Or not even asking the question but simply stating "Burned my finger with boiling hot water—top of the tea kettle fell off" will often elicit such responses as:

> Sorry to hear that—the key is to run it under cold water for 10 minutes—don't use ice! After that, use Neosporin to disinfect and make sure to keep it covered and clean. I did this once, and it will heal in about a week, but it hurts like heck!
> —Sandy

> Don't use ice on it, only cold water. No need to go to the hospital even though I'm sure it looks red and awful.
> —Logan

After their physician, nurse, or pharmacist, people look within their network from those they trust for good advice on medical treatments and medications. In the iCrossing study, more than 60 percent list "Consumer Opinion Leader" as "extremely important" or "very important." Some even list the advice from their friends above that of their physician.[6]

"It's in my doctor's best interest to make money and he does that by performing surgeries or having repeat business. That is why I look to my friends with similar issues for advice. Social media is the quickest, least intrusive and effective way that I know to do this," said Connie Weatherald, 83, of Stuart, Florida.[7]

In the same study, 75 percent indicated that they use social media in health to "connect with other consumers to exchange information or get support"; 55 percent noted that the most important reason to use social media over other online sites is to get cost information for a procedure or medical equipment.[8] Consumer-generated health content is increasing in both supply and demand. Society is benefiting from this shift. Perhaps the largest benefit to this will be seen outside of the United States where in some small towns the local physician is revered as a demigod. This is fine if that physician is altruistic at heart, but that is not always the case. Social media allows for an inexpensive and relevant second, third, and four-hundredth medical opinion especially in underdeveloped regions of the world.

Jared and Subway's Almost Missed Opportunity

Marketers struggling with idea ownership are not doing so entirely because of advances in social media or technology. One of the most successful marketing campaigns of all-time nearly didn't get off the ground. Jared and his Subway weight-loss story did not come from the top down; rather, it came from the bottom up. Jared actually started the now famous diet on his own. The story made its way from a college campus newspaper to a savvy advertising executive. This executive sent an intern to track Jared at the University of Indiana.

The marketing executives at Subway originally rejected the idea, but the ad agency and this particular executive were so convinced of the idea that they sold the idea to local franchisees, and the agency paid to run the spots out of its own pocket! Only after proven success did the marketing executives at Subway's headquarters relent. This turned out to have a happy ending, but how many such ideas have never seen the light of day?

In the Subway campaign, recall that Jared was an avid user of a company's product and service—in this case low-fat submarine sandwiches. This is another reminder that executives and companies that want to excel need to be comfortable in knowing that not everything related to the brand will be owned by them, that their customer is beginning to take ownership. This is a good thing, because straight-forward and true stories resonate well with consumers as evidenced by Subway overtaking McDonald's as having the most restaurants in the United States.

The beauty of social media is that fewer of these great stories will remain hidden, and as a result, companies will benefit. One of the top-10 viral videos in 2008 was "Christian the Lion."[9] This is a clip of two Australian men who raise a lion in the city of London and then go to Africa a year later to reunite in the wild with a giant hug (Remember, this is a Lion!). This story was from 1969 and, despite having a book published about it in 1971 (Broadway Books), prior to 2008it was rel-atively unknown. Then along comes the social medium of YouTube and the story spreads globally in little time at all. Imagine, this incred-ible story would have only been known by a few until the advent of social media—what a shame! Ironically, it has come full circle, and a second book has been published on it: "A Lion Called Christian: The True Story of the Remarkable Bond between Two Friends and a Lion" by Anthony Bourke, John Rendall, and George Adamson (March 10, 2009), and it is on Border's Best Seller's Shelf! This is also an exam-ple of how social media can drive offline revenue in new forms as well.

Not All Applications Are Created Equal

Businesses, both large and small, have to realize that they no longer own relationships. Yet, many companies, when it comes to social media, haven't shaken their old tired-and-true marketing models. Other companies quickly figured it out. Next, we discuss three com-panies that all had the same goal when they set out, but wound up experiencing different levels of success based on their strategies.

In 2007, Facebook introduced the ability for developers to make applications (tools/widgets that allow users to do everything from tracking a favorite sports team's scores to playing a game of tic-tac-toe against a friend in another city) to enhance the Facebook experience. When the application platform was originally introduced, three separate travel companies correctly surmised that people would want to input and track all the places in the world they had visited. Each company set out with different strategies resulting in various levels of success. The three companies were:

1. Where I've Been (a new company)
2. TripAdvisor (a popular online travel agent)
3. ACME Travel (a large, traditional tour operator)

One of the top executives at ACME Travel had a relationship with someone at Facebook and was aware that Facebook was planning to open its application program interface (API) that would allow any company to develop useful widgets within Facebook. For example, Delta Airlines could develop an application in which users could view upcoming flights on Facebook, or Crayola could have you fill out some silly questions and tell you what color crayon you most represent.

ACME Travel thought it would be helpful for the users to be able to easily track where they had traveled. The idea sprang from an employee who had invented an Excel spreadsheet that allowed you to check off boxes next to countries traveled. The idea was a good one because within the first few days hundreds of thousands of Facebook users downloaded the application. Understanding also the braggadocian behavior of social media, ACME Travel set up the application so that people could send an alert to their friends whenever they traveled to a new city. So, if Kim went to Auckland, it would alert everyone in her network "Kim indicated she has traveled to Auckland within ACME's travel application."

ACME Travel was ecstatic at the success of their application; they estimated that the internal cost to build the application was $15,000, and they were receiving 50,000 downloads per day, which means they were capturing 50,000 names to put into their prospect database.[10] To go into this particular aspect a bit further, the download process for Facebook applications doesn't require users to forfeit their e-mail addresses—yet ACME Travel made the decision to place an extra page in the middle of the download process indicating it was mandatory for users to supply name, mailing address, and e-mail address in order to use the application. About a week into the process, ACME received e-mail from one of their users, 20-something Craig Ulliot. He sent a message to ACME Tours suggesting that the additional page during the application download process was cumbersome and would discourage many users who didn't want to disclose personal information to get the application, ultimately hurting the overall success of the application. ACME Tours reviewed the comment from Ulliot and conceded there probably were people they were turning off, but then again, they were getting 50,000 names on some good days, so things were going very nicely. Besides, they thought, this was the entire reason they were doing social media marketing, it was a *carrot* to get names for the database.

Things continued successfully for ACME Travel for a few weeks. Meanwhile, Craig Ulliot wasn't your typical user; rather, he was a very established programmer. He liked the idea of the *mousetrap* that ACME Travel was offering, but he thought he could build a better one. After all, the Web is all about beg, borrow, and make better. So, a few weeks later, he set sail with his own, very similar application, called "Where I've Been." Where I've Been was graphically more appealing and also contained some sexier pieces of flash programming that made it easier to click on a particular part of a map to indicate you'd traveled to a certain place. However, the key difference was that Craig didn't add the additional page during the download process that required you to enter your personal information. He simply used Facebook's standard two-step process. So what do you think happened?

Where I've Been quickly became one of the must-have applications and also the top-downloaded travel application. It was so successful that Craig was able to start a seven-person company under the same name. With 800,000 active monthly users, Craig was attracting the attention of the big online travel agents like TripAdvisor, Priceline, and Travelzoo.

TripAdvisor was savvy enough to realize that an application like this would be an unbelievable marketing tool for their business. TripAdvisor began behind-the-scenes negotiations with Where I've Been. By this time Craig had hired a seasoned Internet travel veteran named Brian Harmon to head up his strategy. The asking price was a little steeper than TripAdvisor had originally hoped. They had hoped that they would be dealing with some wet-behind-the-ears-kid and get the application for a bargain.

They came within a whisker of buying the application for $3 million. So close in fact, that a story was released about it. Then they did something very smart, they did the exact same thing that Craig had done to ACME Travel—they begged, borrowed, and made better.

TripAdvisor pulled back, took a deep breath, and calmly said we think we can do this better. Instead of investing $3 million, they decided to build their own application for a fraction of the cost. Now it's important to point out that TripAdvisor used two very good tactics. The first one was a prudent attempt to leverage an already proven and successful product-application in Where I've Been.

On discovering the expensive asking price, TripAdvisor reassessed the situation and correctly decided there was enough opportunity for more than one company to succeed. With Facebook counting user growth in millions, TripAdvisor was hopeful that this type of travel application had not "jumped the shark." Jumping the shark is an Internet term for something that is past its prime or no longer *in*. According to *Wikipedia* the specific definition is:

> *Jumping the shark* is a colloquialism used by TV critics and fans to denote that point in a TV show or movie series' history where the plot veers off into absurd story lines or out-of-the-ordinary characterizations. In the process of undergoing these changes, the TV or movie series loses its original appeal. Shows that have "jumped the shark" are typically deemed to have passed their peak. According to the theory, once a show has "jumped the shark" fans can designate the point of the show's perceived decline in overall quality with the "jump the shark" moment.[11]

The term was taken from one of the later *Happy Days* episodes where Fonzie, leather jacket and all, attempts to jump a shark on water skis. It was *not* one of broadcast television's finer moments. The tech community eagerly snapped up this television term, and today it is more recognized in the Internet community for the moment that something goes past its prime. For instance most MP3 players had a jump the shark moment when the iPod was first released.

Anyway, TripAdvisor moves forward with building a bigger, better version of Where I've Been. Within a month they released "Cities I've Visited." They are smart to name it something very tangible and "sticky" with cities. TripAdvisor leveraged Google Maps so travelers could place pins on the digital map just like many people do in their home or office on paper maps. Using Google Maps was smart in four ways:

1. People were familiar with Google Maps.
2. Google Maps was free.
3. No development was needed.
4. It worked.

That old adage that you can only have two out of the following—cheap, quick, or quality—doesn't hold true within social media because you are often either leveraging preexisting human capital or preexisting products/solutions. In this instance, TripAdvisor was doing both—they were leveraging the idea (human capital) that Where I've Been and ACME Travel had produced before them, and they were leveraging Google Maps (preexisting product). So, their rough cost investment was around $20,000. What they received in return is somewhat staggering. In April of 2009, TripAdvisor's application had 1,779,246monthly active users, while Where I've Been had 885,577monthly active users.[12] Both were very successful—that's almost 1.8 million people who actively interact with TripAdvisor's brand every month! Craig was able to start an company due to the success of this one application as well. That is truly the power of social media.

A key thing to note is that for every successful Cities I've Visited or Traveler IQ application we had just as many, if not more, not achieve wild success. The importance in a social media age is to be nimble and not afraid to make mistakes. The more things you can test or try, the more chances you have for success. I have a sign outside my door that simply says Speed Wins. We have adopted this as our motto and it serves us well. If our development team says something will take four months, we challenge ourselves to do it in four days, and more often than not we succeed. It may not be perfect for that initial beta launch, but that is okay, because with the help of our users we will make small, rapid changes to constantly improve. If you aren't constantly evolving along with your customers you will be doomed to fail.

—Craig Ulliot

Marketing to Zombies

We introduced the term "active monthly users." This term was introduced by Facebook in 2007 and is an important one. Historically most tracking just dealt with pure volume. How many "hits" did you get on your website? Then it was determined that hits wasn't really relevant since hits were tracking the number of times certain elements on a page were served up. If your website home page had several images and form fields and one person visited this site, her visit could equal 13 hits; this type of count is not too helpful. So, tracking progressed to visits, this wasn't very good either because it could be the same person coming back several times. The next logical step was to measure unique visitors.

Social media has changed the paradigm of tracking again. Originally, Facebook rated top applications by how many times they were downloaded, but downloads aren't necessarily relevant; what truly matters is how active the users are. If a user downloads the application and never returns, that's not very valuable to the creator of the application. If a million people download something but never use it, then in a sense it is worthless to both the user and to the creator. This is why Facebook tracks by active users, which changes everything.

Having 12 million e-mail addresses in your database doesn't mean much if only 1,000 open and click on your e-mails. It's much more important to have 10,000 e-mails with 9,000 people opening and clicking. With social media, marketers are able to tell how active users are as well as such helpful information as age, sex, education, hobbies, interests, and so on. This assists marketers in these one-to-one conversations between companies and consumers.

Going one step further is just how powerful the social graph is. Take for example the 9,000 active people mentioned above. E-mail is generally a one-to-one conversation. If you have an e-mail that contains something particularly entertaining, then you could be lucky and those 9,000 people forward it on, and so forth. This is powerful, but not quite as awesome as social media. The main reason is that the viralness of e-mail is really related to that one particular e-mail, whereas in social media people are constantly pushing content to their network. In e-mail it's an anomaly, whereas in social media it is inherent.

To showcase this point, EF Educational Tours in April of 2009 had roughly 800 people "following" them on Twitter—people who actively wanted to know the latest news from EF Educational Tours. If you looked at the number of followers these 800 people had, then the social graph influence was 8.5 million people (based on results from a query on http://twinfluence.com/).

Leveraging Success

The TripAdvisor story doesn't end with the brand value derived from the application; that was only the beginning. The beauty is that 1.8 million users are feeding TripAdvisor information. These augment their 30 million user base—talk about a large focus group! The days of advertising executives sitting behind two-way mirrors munching on stale chips and M&Ms will become a distant memory. More important than healthier marketers is the opportunity this vast amount of data presents. First of all, companies can provide this data to reporters as part of their public relations efforts. For example: "Top-five cities that people want to travel to in the coming year"—"35 to 45 year olds more likely to travel to Australia—teenagers to Europe."

Reporters and bloggers are always looking for this type of hard data that is of interest to consumers. What they learn real time can also help shape their product and services. The level of demographic information passed within social media is unprecedented. If TripAdvisor sees in October that 80 percent of males 55 to 65 are putting Machu Picchu as a place they desire to visit when historically only 20 percent select that destination, then it would make intuitive sense to change the TripAdvisor home page to have a callout for a Machu Picchu Senior's special. This is where marketers' jobs are changing drastically. This data is being collected from the web site, as well as all the social media touchpoints.

Marketers need to be joined at the hip with their production team to ensure they are getting this real-time information. They also need to recognize that they are no longer sending a one-way message but are serving more as a conduit. "Those who will succeed need to act more like publishers, entertainment companies, or even party planners, than advertisers,"[13] says Garrick Schmitt, Group Vice President of Experience Planning for leading digital agency Razorfish.

The process TripAdvisor employed building the "Cities I've Visited" application is a new way of thinking in that TripAdvisor didn't know for certain what they would be able to monetize. "Users are challenging publishers, advertisers, and marketers to meet their needs in new, distributed and largely uncharted territories—many of which have no analog touch points—and to provide services that have no immediate monetization models,"[14] indicated Schmitt.

It's also a circular communication cycle. In this case, if someone within the "Cities I've Visited" application selects Athens under the category "I'd like to visit," then TripAdvisor has the ability to serve up its top-five most popular tours of Athens (which of course are clickable) to that user to take him directly into a booking process at the appropriate point in time. It's easy to see why this isn't interruption marketing like in days gone past; but it is a value-added part of a useful tool for the user. TripAdvisor is offering value to this Athens user in providing a tool to track and brag about where he's gone as well as where he'd like to go, and at the same time, the user is receiving valuable information from TripAdvisor that is directly tied to his particular travel interests. There is no marketing guesswork or marketing laboratory—the user is informing marketers implicitly though his actions.

Companion Credit Union: New Logo

One Australian company, Companion Credit Union, actually turned over the decision on its brand logo to the social community. "The credit union is really owned by the members, and therefore, we decided we should invite them to actively participate in helping us decide."[15] said Ray O'Brien, CEO/Companion. Of the 12,000 members, 1,000 of them voted. "Many of our current members founded Companion Credit Union, so it only seemed fitting that they would be a part of our new journey and direction," said Companion's Marketing Manager Cas Scott.[16]

E-Books

Mobile devices acting as e-book readers (Amazon Kindle, Sony eReader, Apple iPod, etc.) are becoming wildly popular (one of the top-selling gifts for Christmas 2008) and the fact is that online books offer many of the same advantages as digitized music, newspapers, and magazines. The *New York Times* is available via eReader for a monthly subscription fee that is drastically less than the traditional paper edition.

It is only a matter of time before we will see advertising and marketing efforts creep into both fiction and nonfiction materials. This is virgin territory for marketers. This is a good thing because as the traditional channels of marketing like television, radio, and magazines diminish in effectiveness, marketers need these new marketing outlets to continue to thrive. One way in which marketers, publishers, and authors will come together as it relates to e-books is within the content itself. How is this possible without compromising the story? On some levels, this is very simple. Let's say that within a scene of a novel the author describes a hot, dusty day where the main character refreshes himself with an ice cold Coca-Cola. Authors generally like to describe items specifically so the reader can really visualize them. That is why more often than not they use branded items in their descriptions—they don't write "soda," they write "Coca-Cola"; they don't write "listening to an MP3 player," they write "listening to an iPod"; and last but not least, they don't write "a stylish Swedish over-the-shoulder baby carrying device," they keep it short with "Baby Bjorn." Because of this, there is tremendous potential for advertisers and authors alike as e-books continue their rise in popularity.

In the previous example, if there is a mention of Baby Bjorn, the company can pay to have that mention become a hyperlink within the e-book's digital format. The benefits of this are that it makes the brand term more pronounced, and if the reader is inclined, he or she can click on the term and either be given more description, branding, or an image or taken directly to babybjorn.com. Another benefit to Baby Bjorn is that the search engine spiders will read its hyperlink, which will help Baby Bjorn come up high in the search rankings.

Where in the World Is Bangladesh?

Thinking outside of brands entirely—books often mention a geographic location. With traditional books, curious readers will look up places like Transylvania with maps or mapping tools to learn where it is. With e-books this is made simple because it is only one click away, and that click takes you straight to the location on a digital map. So, e-books provide a benefit to the reader. Think of a particular word in a novel that you may not know the meaning of—say "panoply." Rather than having to look up panoply in the dictionary, the definition would be one click a way or you may even be able to mouse over it with the cursor to see a pop-up definition. Both of these can be monetized by the publisher and author. Google already generates revenue from its mapping application, so it makes sense that a business development could be struck that Google be the preferred provided of mapping information within books; in return, the publisher or author receives a portion of the revenue that Google generates.

Going back to the brand-product-placement-within-a-book scenario, you could argue that if the author is already placing brand terms into her book (e.g., Coke), then why would a company like Coke pay for something that is already there. Coke would want to do this for two reasons: (1) the competition (Pepsi) could swoop in and take this placement, or (2) the placement isn't currently a hyperlink in the e-book, but by paying a small sponsorship fee, the company could make it a hyperlink thus driving traffic and helping improve organic search engine rankings (because search engines reward hyperlinks).

If all of this makes so much sense, why haven't they had this type of product placement in books before now? It wasn't feasible primarily because of tracking. An advertiser wouldn't be able to track the effectiveness of this form of product placement in a book. Now, with product placements in e-books you will be able to see how many people viewed (millions of impressions) along with how many people clicked or moused over the word with their cursor. This is great for advertisers and even better for the authors and publishers who now have an additional revenue stream without compromising their content, but rather enhancing it for their readers. It will be interesting to see how advertisers will be charged for these types of placements; the most logical would probably be a cost-per-thousand-impressions model.

While the transition from both hardcover and paperback to electronic versions will occur, and we are at the beginning of that trail. It will not be as rapid or absolute a succession as other industries (e.g., music, movies). Rather e-books will be complements or alternatives. Part of this is because there is something more genuine and romantic about curling up with a good book. It's not quite the same if you are curling up with your electronic reading device. Another factor is that books are one of the most viral offline items that exist today. Books, especially paperbacks, are disposable—passed from friend to friend; owners don't really plan to ever see the book again. Also, with today's technology, it is still 25 percent faster to read something on a piece of paper than it is to read from a computer screen, let alone a smaller handheld e-book reader. Unlike music and news content, the content within books is not as time sensitive, especially for fiction. The shelf life for a book is much longer than news content or the popularity of a song. A salient example of this is the fact that today middle school kids are still reading *Huckleberry Finn* and *The Catcher in the Rye*. In the foreseeable future, while e-books will be exceedingly popular, they will be more of a complement than an absolute replacement like the music and newspaper/magazine industry has experienced.

For publishers there are both pros and cons to the book-publishing model being influenced by the rise of e-books. On one hand, publishers potentially save millions of dollars on physical printing and shipping of inventory and they would have an additional revenue stream in terms of the advertising/hyperlink placements within the e-books. On the other hand, they are "middleman," which may not be as crucial a role when an author can get his or her content directly to the reading audience easily (a good example of this is Google Books allowing authors and publishers to upload their content in PDF format. Google was sued and did lose a court battle because more than one proprietary owner didn't want their content placed on Google Books).

Unlike the music and movie industry, the book industry has thrived even though for hundreds of years there has been a free alternative to purchasing a book, public libraries. It will be interesting see how the public library model morphs to address e-books. The book industry still thrives in spite of the free availability of the same content at the public library for many reasons: (1) people like to own books; (2) it takes an effort to go to the library, check out a book, and then remember to return it on time; (3) library books have return dates; and (4) there are often long waiting lists for new books. With e-book technology, it is possible that hurdles 2, 3, and 4 from the previous list will go away entirely. Specifically, there is no need to go to the library because the content can be wirelessly pushed or downloaded to the e-book device direct from the Library. Also, once you have the e-book, you don't have a time limit in which to return it. As for the waiting list for the more popular books, because there is no physical item/inventory (i.e., the book itself), it is limitless; theoretically everyone in the world can read the book at the same time.

Libraries will need to set up some sort of licensing agreement in the short term with publishers when it comes to e-books. So, there may not be limitless inventories and time lines for e-books for libraries. For example, if you want to read *The Da Vinci Code* as an e-book from the Library, the Library may only have the rights to five e-book copies at a time, and the content may automatically expire from your e-book reader in 30 days. The good news is that inventory will be easier to track (no more lost books) saving the taxpayer some money because libraries will be less costly to maintain. In the long run though, the best model would not have any restrictions, but would be limitless because the more information is free and available, the more society benefits.

Chapter Five Key Points

1. Consumers are looking to peers for recommendations on products, services, health issues, and more via social media. Only companies that produce great products and services will be part of these conversations; mediocrity will quickly be eliminated. Today, 76 percent rely on what others say, while 15% rely on advertising.[17]
2. Social media helps eliminate different people performing the same tasks (multiple individual redundancies) resulting in a more efficient society.
3. The old adage that you can only have two of these—cheap, quick, or quality—doesn't hold true within social media. It's possible to have all three.
4. Successful companies in social media will function more like entertainment companies, publishers, or party planners rather than as traditional advertisers.
5. With the increasing popularity of e-books there will be new digital media placement opportunities for brands. This is very similar to product placement in movies, only this is for books, and the placements are clickable and trackable.
6. The most successful social media and mobile applications

are those that allow users to brag, compete, or look cool by passing it on.7. The main threat to Google in the search wars is not another search engine, but the rise of search queries within social media.

Chapter Six

Death of Social Schizophrenia

If you are Generation X or older you have most likely spent most of your life in a schizophrenic* world. You took on a different role or character depending on where you were or who you were with. Most of us had at least two personas; normally a work persona and a non-work persona. And, many had several personas: social, work, family, coach, charity, and so on.

For instance, your behavior at an event like Woodstock or Burning Man was much different than at the office the following Monday. "Al the Accountant" may only be known by his coworkers as "Meticulous Accountant Al"; while his bowling pals would know him only as "Al-Valanche," because you better get out of the way when he is partying otherwise you could be the next victim of the "Al-Valanche."

Even if you believe that life with social media is worse, you cannot argue that social media has forever changed the way in *which* we live.

In 2008, North Carolina's All-American basketball player Tyler Hansbrough found himself in the middle of a media whirlwind. Hansbrough was a hard-nosed player and the poster child of all that is good about college basketball. Because of his intensity, he was nick-named Psycho T.

One sunny day in Chapel Hill, Hansbrough was hanging out with some friends at a fraternity house off campus. With some encouragement, Hansbrough thought it would be a thrill to launch his 6'10" 260-pound body into the fraternity swimming pool. The thrill part being

*Schizophrenia is a very serious illness and our intent by the use of this term is not to make light of its serious conditions or those who suffer from this illness.

that he was jumping off the roof located three stories up. Now this type of behavior has been going on for decades from nonstudent athletes and student athletes alike. However, on this particular day, one of the observers captured a video of Hansbrough's behavior on his smartphone.

Once this video became known to the general media, North Carolina's Head Basketball Coach (Roy Williams) had to make a difficult decision about whether to suspend Hansbrough or not. Because drinking wasn't involved and Hansbrough was a model student athlete, he made the tough decision not to suspend Hansbrough. Helping Hansbrough's cause was his modus operandi of being intense—after all Psycho T was just being Psycho T. If this had taken place five years ago, Coach Williams and Hansbrough would have never found themselves in such a predicament. Boys would be boys, and no one would have known about it, and life would have continued.

Psycho T being Psycho T is a good example of the new world not having as many casual schizophrenics. People are best off being comfortable in their own skin and not pretending to be anything that they aren't. Well-known author Marcus Buckingham's (*Now Discover Your Strengths*) philosophy of playing to your strengths is further played out in a social media world. Transparency demands it, and with so much information flowing this way and that, it is extremely difficult for a person who is well rounded to stand out in this new world.

Without a doubt, it is somewhat daunting to always be on one's best behavior. It is mentally taxing to have fewer avenues to blow off steam or to always maintain a perfect persona. Perhaps Al the Accountant is more effective at work and dogmatic on the details because outside of work he can let it all go and doesn't have to burden himself with the details.

As a result of preventative and braggadocian behavior, extra curricular activities like music, theatre, and organized sports will become even more popular and important because they provide mechanisms of release for people.

Interactive games like Second Life and Sims were big for a while, and then their popularity started to wane. These games allow users to create fictional personas (often in the form of what is called an avatar) in computerized virtual worlds. These types of games can potentially make a comeback because it has become increasingly difficult for people to take on another character/persona in the real world.

Or perhaps these simulation games will experience a quick death because people may find it difficult to brag about playing a simulated game that replicates life instead of just leading their own lives. Also, these games may be too transparent. A high school teacher can't simply take on the persona of a hooker specializing in sadomasochism without realizing long-term ramifications when this eventually becomes known. In fact, schools have terminated several teachers for this type of unacceptable social media behavior. After all, there is a high degree of probability that the teacher could run into one of his or her students within the virtual world as well. A happy medium may be social video games, which are already wildly popular. If I'm going to spend 60 minutes on the bike at the gym, it's much more exiting if I'm competing against digital avatars of people I know and don't know at other gyms, and even more exciting if there is a celebrity rider like Lance Armstrong who also happens to be on a stationary bike in Austin, Texas while I'm in Cambridge, Massachusetts.

While there are downsides to such 24 x 7 personal openness; overall, it's easy to take the side of arguing that appropriate transparency is in sum a good thing for individuals and society. It is without question much "cooler" to say you are bungee jumping off a remote mountain pass overhang in New Mexico than updating your status with "I'm watching the latest adventure reality series." Imagine a world that reintroduces people to living their own realities, rather than watching someone else's. Maybe this is why simulation games like Second Life haven't been as wildly successful as many pundits predicted; perhaps people have come to the realization that in reality (pun intended) it is much cooler to lead their own lives.

One of the more overt examples of the downside of not being yourself within social media is the sad case of Lori Drew. Lori was concerned that her daughter's friend, a 13-year-old named Megan Meier, was mistreating her daughter, Sara. So, Lori decided to set up a

MySpace account pretending to be an attractive teenage boy named Josh Evans. Josh flirted with Megan and eventually they became social media buddies and developed an online relationship. Once the "hook was set" the persona of Josh then started berating Megan through a series of unfriendly comments and nasty remarks. These remarks proved too much for Megan, who had a history of battling depression, and one day she hung herself. At the time, Lori Drew (a 49-year-old Missouri mom) faced three years in prison and a $300,000 fine for an online harassment campaign that resulted in the suicide of a teenage girl. More laws are being enacted to curtail cyberbullies like Lori Drew.

Even Football Players Need to Calm Down

A Texas Longhorn offensive lineman found out the hard way the importance of preventative behavior in social media. The lineman posted a racist update on his Facebook profile just after Barack Obama was elected president of the United States: "all the hunters gather up, we have a #$%& in the whitehouse."[1]

Soon after that was posted, Coach Mack Brown kicked the lineman off the team. The lineman was unable to participate in Texas' 2009 bowl game. The lineman posted an apology to anyone his comment had offended, but the damage had already been done:

> Clearly I have made a mistake and apologized for it and will pay for it. I received it as a text message from an acquaintance and immaturely put it up on Facebook in the light of the election. I'm not racist and apologize for offending you. I grew up on a ranch in a small town where that was a real thing and I need to grow up. I sincerely am sorry for being ignorant in thinking that it would be okay to write that publicly and apologize to you in particular. I have to be more mature than to put the reputation of my team at stake and to spread that kind of hate which I don't even believe in. Once again, I sincerely apologize.[2]

Meanwhile on another football team, Colorado Head Coach Dan Hawkins instituted the following rule for his players:

If I request to see your page, you'd better let me in and let me see it. Everybody's kind of got their own standards. I tell them if your mom can see it, and neither you nor she is embarrassed, then it's okay. But if your mom can't look at it, then it's probably not right.[3]

Even the cheerleaders need to learn how to behave correctly in this newly opened society. A New England Patriots Professional Cheerleader was kicked off the cheer squad for inappropriate photo postings on her Facebook page. She and her friends went out on a wild drinking binge. When one of her friends passed out they decided to write all over her half-naked body. They drew penises and other lewd symbols along with phrases like "I'm a Jew" and swastika symbols. They posted and shared these images of their crazy night with their friends.[4]

As a result of these examples and more, NFL teams started engaging in a controversial practice for the 2009 draft. Personnel from respective NFL teams (Packers, Lions, etc.) started creating "fake" Facebook accounts. Most of these profiles were designed to look like they were those of young, energetic and attractive females. The purpose was to become friends with potential draft picks so that the teams could conduct further research. Historically, NFL companies spend hundreds of thousands of dollars on background investigations prior to paying a young college kid millions of dollars. This progression into social media subterfuge only makes sense for them. Just like a regular employer, what they are looking for is anything that could be viewed as detrimental. In some instances they have seen drug posts and gambling items on the college player's profile.

The ethical nature of these football teams creating fake profiles to bait 20-year old athletes can certainly be questioned, but the key point that I will constantly harp on is don't put anything on social media that you don't want the whole world to know about, because eventually, one way or another, the world will know about it.

Just like athletic programs, governments around the world are struggling to determine how to handle some social media issues.

Twenty-two-year-old Croatian Niksa Klecak was picked up by police and interrogated after starting a Facebook group critical of Prime Minister Ivo Sanander. The group was dubbed "I bet I can find 5,000 people who dislike Sanander."[5] The interrogation drew sharp criticism from Croatia's opposition Social Democrat Party and has inspired a host of copycat Facebook groups.

Just as companies have discovered, perhaps the best tactic is not censorship, but rather to address the problem and or have enough good karma produced that it overwhelms and drowns out the negative. Obama's election campaign is a good example of overwhelming good social media vibes drowning out the negativity of the various opposition groups.

Be the Best at Something, Not Everything

As previously discussed, the transparency and speed of information flow caused by social media mitigates casual schizophrenic behavior. This is generally a positive result because maintaining different personas is stressful, exhausting, and disingenuous.

The same holds true for corporate behavior in social media. For corporations, trying to be too many things to too many people is costly. Historically, we have seen the "we are the best at everything" messaging come out of many marketing departments. The marketers always start off with high hopes of simply highlighting one message in a 30-second commercial, but by the end of production, they have flooded the spot with numerous messages. The original intent of an advertiser may be to convey the message, "We have been in the business for 45 years."

However, the end product is often something similar to: "We have been in the business for 45 years, we have the lowest prices, and we have the largest selection. Our brand name *Perfect* is the most trusted, and you can find us at great retailers like Sam's, Costco, and BJ's."

In a 140-character world, if you want to have a chance at helping the consumer retain something and eventually pass it on, it is imperative that you hyperfocus on your strengths or particular niche. There is also a need for continuous flow of information across the entire organization; in particular, it is mission critical for production and marketing to be feeding information back and forth. It's one thing for marketing to respond to consumers' complaints, it's an entirely different thing to respond to the customers complaint, look for trends in product deficiencies, and work closely with production to develop solutions.

The role of a marketer today and in the future has less to do creating 30 Super Bowl spots and guessing what jingle will resonate with prospects and more to do with having ongoing external conversations with the customer/prospects while at the same time having ongoing internal conversations with operations, customer care, and product development.

In turn, production and development will be less about being in a "behind doors" laboratory and will have more to do with being connected with marketing; they too, will have an ongoing dialogue with the customer. Two prime examples of production personnel in 2008 that have the dual roll of product vision and being a public face to the organization are Dave Morin of Facebook and Matt Cutts of Google. At developer conferences, Dave and Matt are almost at the level of rock stars, and they have become the faces of their respective organizations in the development community. They aren't behind closed doors trying to figure out the next best thing for their target audience, they are in constant contact with their target audience and a large part of their role is also marketing. These are two great examples of what marketers will look like in this socialnomic era.

One Message

Companies that engage in brand marketing have always known that it is best to keep the message simple and convey one salient point. Some companies were able to adhere to this principle like 7UP's "Uncola" campaign or FedEx's "When it absolutely positively has to get there overnight" campaign. However, many companies have struggled with this concept. Most often they get myopic—this stuff is so great we need to get it out there—or they get internal pressure from too many executives trying to get their particular interest across.

Companies are lucky if the advertising they create gets remembered at all by the customer, let alone the key message. So when a car company crams in that they have the best miles per gallon, horsepower, and stereo, and they list all the special promotional lease offers with an accompanying disclaimer and then add all the local dealer names at the end of a 30-second commercial, all they are doing is causing mass confusion for the viewing audience. Even when marketing teams know they are supposed to stick to one message; companies often fail because it is tough with all these different elements and parties involved—too many cooks in the kitchen spoil the broth.

The beauty and curse of a 140-character world is that there is no longer a choice. Tony Blair indicated at the 2008 World Business Forum in New York, "Because of the proliferation and speed of information, people and the press want everything in succinct and easy to digest packages. However, some very complex problems can't be put that way. It is quite an extraordinary challenge."[6] Whether we like it or not, or if it is right or if it is wrong, we have to adapt to communication in succinct and salient sound bites.

From production and strategic positioning standpoints, the beauty is that it forces companies to improve. If your company or product can't definitively state what it stands for and how you differ in a few short words, then it is time to reevaluate exactly what you are doing. If you don't have a niche position in a marketplace that you are attempting to defend from your competition, and you are trying to be all things to all people, then you are doomed to failure.

This destructive behavior may have taken longer to figure out in the past because the marketing mediums available allowed advertisers to cram in many different benefits in the hope that so many great things would entice consumers to buy. This was also during a time when customers were more willing to be "spoken to" rather than have a "conversation with." They may have bought your product based solely on the glitz and glamour of your marketing. This possibility is very limited now that we are living in a world with social media.

The good news is that in this new world order, once you have determined your initial messaging strategy you have the ability to reevaluate and tweak it for relevancy based on feedback from the marketplace. Because you will be engaging in a conversation with your customer, you will be able to identify and adapt to changing needs much quicker. That's why it's important to ensure your marketers and production teams are on the same page.

Marketer's Philosophy Yesterday

- It's all about the sex and sizzle of the message and brand imagery.
- It's all about the message; good marketers can sell anything.
- We know what is right for the customer - we are doing the customer a service because they really don't know what they want.
- We develop products and messaging in house and then disperse them to the public.

Marketer's Philosophy Today

- It's important to listen and respond to customer needs.
- It's all about the product; it's necessary to be in constant communication with all other departments.
- We never know what is exactly right for the customer; that is why we are constantly asking and making adjustments, because we usually don't get it right the first time.
- Often our customers will market the product better than we can; if we can leverage one of their ideas, then it is beneficial to everyone.

Referral Program on Steroids

If you were to ask chief marketing officers (CMOs) of varying businesses ranging in size from the Fortune 500 companies to small business owners, what their top performing channels or programs are, the majority would indicate that their referred customers are the most valuable. "Top performers" being defined in terms of return on investment (cost to acquire said customer) as well as the quality of the customer acquired.

The logical follow-up question for the CMOs—what is the greatest challenge you face? The response would again focus on referrals, only it would be fixated on the difficulty in obtaining mass volume from this lucrative channel—"how can we get more?"

For the first time, social media enables corporations and marketers to generate this desired mass scale from the existing customer base.

In the 1990s and continuing into the twenty-first century, Jeff Bezos and Amazon have done a stellar job of introducing the concept of affinity marketing to millions worldwide. For example, when you purchase a DVD or book from Amazon, Amazon gives real-time suggestions of what you might like based on your own prior purchases.

Millions have found this feature to be very helpful, and it has taken us into an appropriate progression in marketing. However, as many have also learned, there are a few pieces to this program that are suboptimal—such as, if you purchase a gift for your four-year-old niece under your own Amazon account. While your niece may enjoy suggestions to buy My Little Pony or American Doll, you as an adult aren't often in the market for such items.

Much more helpful and useful was Amazon's introduction of the ability to showcase to users: "People who purchased this book also purchased these other ones." Here's where social media comes in and takes this one giant step further. In the Amazon model just described, you don't know the other people that are referenced. They are an aggregation of thousands of others who happen to have the same purchasing patterns. In other words, there is no personal connection between you and them. The only shared connection is that you *might* share similar buying habits.

In socialommerce, you still have this same aggregate data made available to you by the Amazons and RedEnvelopes of the world; "here's what the total universe enjoys." But, in socialommerce it goes significantly deeper to show "here's what your specific network enjoys." Within your network, you will begin to identify a handful of friends, possibly more, who seem to have similar tastes and opinions that you can trust. The circle that you trust for recommending movies may be entirely different from the circle you trust for restaurant recommendations.

For example, when you see on your favorite social media tool that your friend Angie—who normally purchases and reads romance novels—has purchased and begun reading a science fiction novel (there are already social media applications and widgets that do exactly this), you might scratch your head and think it quite odd that Angie would be reading such a thing. However, then Angie's recommendation and write-up on the science fiction book pops up a few days later on your updates, and you are quickly enlightened about this oddity: "For those who know me well, you may be surprised to see that I just completed a science fiction piece. This was quite a diversion from my usual romance novel obsession—but let me tell you it was a refreshing one. Thanks goes to my husband who is an avid sci-fi fan; when he came across this book and read it, he thought I would like it—and right he was! I loved it. I highly recommend this book and can say it's one of the best I've read in the past three years."

Now as a good friend of Angie's who shares very similar tastes when it comes to reading, how likely is it that you are going to want to read this book? My guess is pretty likely. You are definitely more apt to give it a try than if you had seen the *exact same* write-up on Amazon.com by someone you didn't know; someone that you didn't identify with or trust immediately.

Then there is Angie; she has a reputation to uphold within her network. If it were a blind review process—like Amazon or Yahoo movies, she is less likely to put as much thought into it as she will for her own network. Spelling a word incorrectly isn't quite as taboo for Angie if it's not going to those who know her and are close to her. If you are debating between giving a particular movie between three and four stars and you have some sort of identity immunity, studies have shown that you are more likely to give four stars. Whereas if your review is going to your friends, you will be more likely to be conservative and give it three stars. This is somewhat intuitive because you would never want to be the cause of a friend's bad evening at the show; rather you would rather under promise and over deliver.

Of course this concept of sharing and reviewing among friends isn't new—book clubs have been around for years. The difference is that book clubs meet once per month and will continue to do so. The need for book clubs doesn't go away. However with social media, information is shared daily and about much more than the just the single book that was assigned. It also allows others to be involved who can't make it to traditional book clubs for myriad reasons, geographical limitations, family commitments, job demands, and so on.

So, what does this change mean for companies exactly? It means that many of their dreams have become realities—"If only we could get more referrals"—well, the referral floodgates have been opened my friends. However, companies should always be careful what they wish for. Great companies that already produce great content, products, or services welcome the frontier of socialnomics with open arms. While they are not guaranteed continued success, they are certainly positioned for it. Meanwhile, those companies that have survived to date by being great at "middleman games"—whether it is distribution related, direct mail, brand marketing, lobbying, public relations, or legal rights—will have a greater challenge in front of them. This challenge must be taken on immediately to secure survival.

Where these companies have staked their fortunes has been with the "the middleman." Well the middlemen are becoming less important than they've been in the past, and the rise in power is shifting rapidly to the social graph. This was no more evident than in the 2008 race for the Democratic Party presidential candidate (more on page 000) where a little-known Senator from Illinois was able to defeat one of histories great "political machines"—Hillary Clinton. This type of historic victory would have been extremely difficult to architect without the Obama camp having the ability to understand and to leverage the power and advantage that socialnomics brings. In this instance, the "Clinton Political Machine" was the item that had lost some of its power, and that power was transferred to the social graph.

Chapter Six Key Points

1. The transparency and speed of information exchanged within social media mitigates casual schizophrenic behavior. Having a "work" personality and having a "party" personal-

ity will soon become extinct. People and companies will need to have one essence and be true to that essence.

2. Being "well rounded" as a company or individual is less beneficial. It's more productive to play to your core strength. This differentiates you from the competition.

3. Companies that produce great products and services rather than companies that simply rely on great messaging will be winners in a socialnomic world. The social graph is the world's largest and most powerful referral program.

4. Marketers' jobs have changed from creating and pushing to one that requires listening, engaging, and reacting to potential and current customer needs.

Chapter Seven

Winners and Losers in a 140-Character World

Today there are some very popular web sites that reduce or make URLs tiny so that people can fit them within their social media postings, which often have character limits. These tools take a URL string of roughly 100 characters and condense it down to 15, making the URL "tiny." This is necessary in today's "soundbite" society and is a reflection of a societal shift from the languid days of sipping lemonade on front porches to multitasking in Wi-fi enabled Starbucks. In a world where everything becomes condensed and hyperaccelerated, who emerges as winners and losers? In this section, we will explore several case studies that shed light on what it takes to succeed in the world of socialnomics.

Does ESPN Have ESP?

Some savvy entrepreneurs at ESPN in 2008 were ahead of the curve in recognizing the different fundamentals of socialnomics. Their success was the result of innovation and necessity. Fantasy Football's popularity was growing rapidly. In 2008, ESPN started to dedicate more of its television programming to discuss pertinent events related to Fantasy Football; but it still wasn't enough. Fantasy Football experts Matthew Berry and Nate Ravitz knew that the public hungered for more and approached the ABC/ESPN brass. Their plea for more Fantasy Football airtime proved successful.

Although they were not granted airtime or support, they were given the green light to produce their own podcast, *Fantasy Football Today,* which quickly became one of the top-20 most downloaded podcasts within the Apple iTunes store. This was a great achievement, but they were still moonlighting and hadn't produced any revenue that would spark ESPN's attention for more support. This is when they embarked on two very innovative facets and, whether knowingly or not, they were engaging in socialnomic activity. These two facets were actually making the sponsors part of the show's content and also allowing listeners to help produce some of the content as well.

As a result of their rapid ascent in the iTunes download rankings, *Fantasy Football Today* started to draw the attention of some savvy, big-time marketers. Their first sponsor included the feature film *Eagle Eye*. This movie featured Shia LaBeouf and was produced by Steven Spielberg. Aside from covering the latest in Fantasy Football, Berry and Ravitz would often touch on pop culture, including commenting on the popular 1990's television show *Beverly Hills 90210* as well as the *New 90210*.

The podcast varied in length from 15 to 30 minutes depending on how much news they had to cover. The varying lengths of the podcasts are an important item to note and a reflection of how our world is changing. Radio and television broadcasts historically attempt to fill an allotted slot of time. That isn't the case with podcasts. If a podcast only has 16 minutes of newsworthy items to cover, then why waste the commentators' and viewers' time trying to fill the slot with subpar content?

The fact that *Fantasy Football Today* was able to secure a sponsor for the podcast wasn't innovative—this was inevitable once they began to attract a vast audience of listeners. We have seen this type of sponsorship in various podcasts. Another good example is the technology podcast, CNET's *Buzz Out Loud*. Recognized as one of the most popular podcasts in 2008[1] covering Internet and Technology news, it also played up the fact that its segments were "indeterminate length." Its popularity was well deserved because the information was delivered in a concise, but humorous fashion and all angles were covered. Although they were successful in securing big-name sponsors including Best Buy, they adopted an "old paradigm" format when it came to their advertising model that has proven to be a failure. They played a commercial in the beginning, middle, and end of the podcast. Just like in the television world, it was not integrated but rather interruptive; this is disruptive to the listening audience. Worse, for seven months straight Best Buy played the same exact commercial! Please keep in mind that the podcast listening audience is not made up of casual listeners. People don't simply flip through channels and land on something of interest. This podcast is downloaded daily, so many of their loyal listeners are the same from podcast to podcast.

What a wasted opportunity for Best Buy! They could have taken advantage of the glowing personalities of the hosts (Natalie Del Conte, Tom Merrit, Jason Howell) and adjusted the messaging daily by having the hosts read or incorporate the messaging into the show as they saw appropriate. Instead, Best Buy took its terrestrial radio spot and plopped it right in the middle of the show.

Stop the Charade—Nobody Is Perfect

Conversely let's look what the ESPN guys did with their sponsor, *Eagle Eye*. As we mentioned, getting a sponsor for the podcast wasn't innovative, rather it was the way in which they seamlessly incorporated it into the show, often in a tongue-in-cheek fashion. Matthew Berry was on the "single scene" at the time, and the running joke was that he couldn't get a girl to date him. Occasionally, he would even chide himself. Around the release date of the *Eagle Eye* movie, Berry kept with this shtick and dropped comments like "even if this movie is terrible, you should go see it to pay homage to Michelle Monaghan's hotness." A comment like that would often lead into a few other comments about what movies she was in and so on. This was all done without disrupting the flow of the football-themed show. Often these tangents by Berry were about various female celebrities' attractiveness quotient—which wasn't a stretch because the listening audience was 90 percent beer-swilling males. The hosts would even give candid feedback and comments after watching the movie and discussing what they liked and didn't like about the film.

The sponsor, the movie producers of *Eagle Eye*, were also engaging in some basic principals of socialnomics by allowing the hosts to say what they thought about the movie even if it included negative phrases like "even if this movie is terrible." This was a very smart move. By pointing out your flaws, people will give more credence when you point out your strengths. If you try to present yourself or you company as always being perfect, then the listening audience will suspect what you have to say isn't completely true.

Certainly a movie is a simpler product to incorporate into a show without it being too intrusive. But the Fantasy Football podcast followed up with an even greater success—their subsequent sponsor, Charles Schwab. It's difficult to find anything invigorating to say about a financial company, especially during a 2008 financial meltdown, but this podcast was able to deliver the Charles Schwab message brilliantly. The whipping boy on the show was the producer, aptly nicknamed "Pod Vader" (a takeoff on Darth Vader) who was constantly hazed by the hosts for killing the show by virtue of his incompetence. In one of the early podcasts, while they played a robotic-sounding device that answered yes or no questions, they dubbed the robotic voice "Chuck" because the advertising slogan at the time for Charles Schwab was "Talk to Chuck." They even had a running shtick that Pod Vader was Chuck and that Chuck was Pod Vader.

A typical show during this time went something like this:

Nate: Willie Parker is listed as questionable for this week's game and the Pittsburgh Gazette reports that his backup, Maurice Moore, is most likely to start. So if you have Parker, you may want to pick up his backup Moore, because Parker will most likely not be able to play.

Berry: Yes, but the Steelers are going against the Ravens and the number 1-rated run defense. So, you may be better off picking up Dominic Rhodes of the Colts instead of Parker.

Nate: I disagree; **let's ask Chuck. Chuck** don't you feel that Moore is a better choice than Rhodes.

Synthesized voice: No.

Nate: Okay, **Chuck** has spoken. Now it's time to read some e-mail from our listeners. This one comes from Fred in St.

Louis, and he asks, "Should I trade Roy Williams for Larry Johnson? If it helps my chances of you reading this e-mail on air, I went and signed up for a **Charles Schwab** checking account after hearing you guys say I can earn **3 percent interest.**"

Berry: It does help because **Chuck** knows when to **buy low** and **sell high** just like the stock market, and in this case, you should sell Roy Williams high because he isn't going to have any more value than he does right now.

Nate: Great job in working in the sponsor.

Berry: Well, I am a company man.

Synthesized voice: **Chuck** says yes.

[Laughter]

Berry: That was Pod Vader not **Chuck** because Pod Vader is **Chuck.**

Pod Vader: No I am not!

[Laughter in the studio . . .][2]

This was brilliant and far different than a traditional 30-second radio advertisement because the sponsor and *Fantasy Football Today* realized their format (daily podcast) is much different than radio advertising—they weren't going to make the same mistake that Best Buy did by running the same spot for seven months straight to the same audience. Instead, creatively incorporating Charles Schwab placement became an integral part of the show without it being intrusive; in fact, you could argue that it enhanced the show by adding a witty element to it. In this case, through creative thinking, the advertiser's involvement actually added content rather than interruption.

Consumers today, in particular Millennials and Generation Zers don't want to be spoken to, they'd rather have conversations and steady ongoing relationships with companies. The callers and e-mailers on the *Fantasy Football Today* show were having fun with the sponsorships by writing them into the show and referencing the sponsors in their e-mails. For example: "I have my **Eagle Eye** on the Packers game this week" and "**Chuck** may know finances, but he was wrong about running back Dominic Rhodes—that chump didn't score a touchdown this week so I am going to **Chuck** him off my fantasy football team this week."

The most Socialnomic piece of all in regards to this *Fantasy Football Today* podcast example is that the advertising wasn't wrapped around the content, but rather was an integral part of it. This is important because when items are passed virally between individuals using social media tools, if the advertisements are on the front or backend of the valuable content or they are banners or display advertisements that float on the periphery of the content, they are too easily stripped/removed when the content is passed from one person to the next. For example, in your company sponsored video on YouTube where banners were to the left and right of the video, when the video was shared among a social network, since the ads aren't in the video itself, only the video would be passed on. Your advertising placement would be eliminated from the string, and you would lose the potential to take advantage of the viral activity.

In Section Three, we discussed a Diet Coke and Mentos example in which you can see that the Diet Coke items and product placement are the actual content itself. It's important to note the dramatic shift that is being propelled by social media. The world around us is shifting from a model where marketers historically have supported content to one in which marketers and companies need to create their own content or seamlessly integrate with existing content. Ironically, this harkens back to the advent of television, when sponsors helped produce the content; soap operas have their name because soap powder companies used to write shows around the use of their product.

Free Labor

In the *Fantasy Football Today* podcast, it would be painfully difficult to try to find every iteration or mention of "Charles Schwab" or "Chuck" because it is actually part of the show—it's not nearly as simple as removing an advertisement that was placed at the front, middle, and end of a broadcast. The second major socialnomic piece that the Football Podcasts at ESPN employed was leveraging the audience base to assist with content. As mentioned, these podcasts needed to be produced at a cost of next to nothing. They weren't getting large financial backing from corporate headquarters; rather, it was sink or swim.

One segment during the week was to report on the various teams across the league. If they had employed the principles of the past, they would have started by using and leveraging existing field reporters (e.g., Sal Paolantonio, Andrea Kramer, John Clayton) who would be sent to the various cities and team camps to learn and report back on the particular happenings of those teams. In this scenario, the shows' producers would receive high-level reporting from experts on a few teams during the week. This is an outrageously expensive model because it includes incurring costs for flights, hotel, and transportation, per diem as well as paying top talent with celebrity-esque salaries easily in the six-figure range. These are costs that the *Fantasy Football Today* podcast could not afford to sustain. As a result, the producers of these podcasts decided to travel down a different path that has resulted in a brilliant revolution in 'news' reporting. Because of its success, we are seeing a shift toward this type of news reporting today.

The producers had people write the show requesting to be the "Super Fan" for their particular team. Many companies attempt to get this level of engagement by giving away a costly contest prize for people who submit their photos with a product, create a video, or write an essay about why they deserve to be a contest winner.

This historically popular giveaway or sweepstakes approach can cause the opposite effect on people submitting entries because it devalues what you are attempting to do and a typical response from a potential contestant may be "oh this company needs to bribe us to submit something and since that prize is of no worth to me, I will *not* submit anything."

The Tom Sawyer Approach

ESPN decided to engage in a route other than a typical sweepstakes model. ESPN didn't have to give anything away, and they had hundreds of applications from fans expressing heartfelt reasons and arguments about why they should be the Super Fan of their particular NFL team. Keep in mind that if they were selected as a Super Fan, then their responsibilities would include weekly check-ins where they were required to report on the current status of their particular teams—they would need to know everything about them. Rather than a sweepstakes prize, the winners would actually be put to work!

This is a monumental step toward leveraging the audience base. ESPN's loyal podcast listeners were begging to do free work! This is analogous to when Tom Sawyer was painting the fence white and made it appear so appealing to those around him that poor saps were hoodwinked into literally begging to have a chance to paint the fence. Tom Sawyer knew that if his approach was "ah come on, if you help me paint this, there is a chance I will buy you some red licorice," it wouldn't be nearly as effective as giving the illusion that painting the fence was a pure joy.

In this instance, these aren't poor saps; the audience has become Jane the Blogger. These are people who have a pressing desire to be heard. They are people who want to be a part of something bigger than themselves. They are also fanatical about their teams, and their teams say something about who they are (similar to brands). A fan of the San Francisco 49ers is more "wine and cheese with a flair for the dramatic" whereas a fan of the Pittsburgh Steelers is more "cheese steak, blue collar and no nonsense."

ESPN leveraged its worldwide platform to ensure that these Super Fans didn't make competing platforms at the local level. It is a proactive way to look at the old saying, "if you can't beat 'em, join 'em." They reversed this old axiom with an approach of "join 'em before they beat you."

During the Super Fan selection process, they even allowed for the audience to help determine the criteria for selection. If your suggestion was taken, then you were automatically named a Super Fan. One of the winning suggestions was that each applicant should have to donate a minimum of $25 to the Jimmy V Foundation for the Fight Against Cancer. So, as part of the application process, submitters were showing receipts to prove that they had in fact donated at least $25.

They picked the best and brightest of the bunch to be the delegated Super Fan for each team. There was a San Diego Chargers Super Fan, Detroit Lions Super Fan, and so on. Whether ESPN knew it or not, they were practicing Socialnomics and utilizing a brilliant strategy that can be summarized in the following four important fronts:

1. The show garnered hundreds of fans who demonstrated their engagement with the show by sending in applications detailing why they should be a Super Fan. Many of the more humorous entries were read on the air even if they weren't picked.

2. They asked their audience what the selection criteria should be and received a recommendation that was better than anything they would have conjured up behind a closed studio door. Specifically, requiring donations to the Jimmy V Foundation for the Fight Against Cancer as part of the application process was a great contribution for a great cause.

3. They avoided paying reporter and travel costs.

4. They could report on all 32 teams during the same week.

5. The Super Fans became expert reporters. As team fanatics, they were able to give a fan perspective on what people cared about. They digested all pieces of media just like Jane the Blogger (page XX) about their particular team. They were a little unpolished in delivery, but since it was a podcast and not live, they could edit it accordingly to glean the appropriate sound bites.

6. ESPN was proactively helping to avoid competition in the future. These individual Super Fans had more than enough knowledge to do a minipodcast on their particular team. By proactively asking them to join, they at least eliminated some of the best potential competition down the road.

7. These 32 Super Fans also have their own social networks that they tell to listen to the show when they are going to be on. "Hey Mom, I know you don't know anything about football, but download this podcast because I'm on it today!"

Point seven isn't a new construct, but it is very powerful with social media. Local newspapers have used this principal for years. The content of the story wasn't half as important as ensuring that it was as crammed with local names—the closer it was to a yellow pages listing, the better. This is a testament to Dale Carnegie's statement that everyone's favorite word in the English language is his or her own name! ESPN realized, just like Dale Carnegie, that if they took on 32 new helpers, those 32 new helpers would be excited to spread the word to their respective social graphs.

While ESPN gets an A, they don't get an A+. One thing they will learn in time is that it's difficult for a host like Berry to perform double duty in the socialnomic age. At the time of this writing, Berry was doing both Fantasy Baseball and Fantasy Football podcasts. Since the respective seasons have crossover, it is virtually impossible for him to be as knowledgeable as the users demand for either baseball or football. Some of these fantasy fans are fanatic for just one sport. If you can't convey to them that you are more expert than they are, then they will tune out or may even decide that they could do a better podcast! In our new niche world, Berry should focus on just one sport, because his audience and future competition will.

Everybody Wants His or Her 15 Minutes of Fame

Another good example of a company effectively using the Tom Sawyer Approach is CNN (iStory and Twitter). CNN anchor Rick Sanchez was an early adopter of harnessing the power of the social graph. Recognizing the huge potential of microblogging, Sanchez became an avid user of the leading technology of the time—Twitter. Twitter's main function allows users, in 140 characters or less, to update people who are following them about what they are doing by using various interfaces (Twitter web site, Twitter modules for iGoogle, Facebook, Yahoo, etc.) Usage ranges from business, "Great article on Southwestern Airlines earnings release can be found here www.abc.com" to the inane, "Just had my fifth Starbucks Pumpkin Spice Venti!" In the beginning, the most popular way people updated their *tweets* was via their mobile phones. Sanchez decided to test out the new medium and began placing his daily activities online.

Obviously some of his activities: "Briefing about Colin Powell interview tonight; just learned that he may disclose some new and interesting information about Barack Obama" are much more interesting than a friend informing you that he is hopped up on pumpkin-flavored Starbucks. Rick was probably pleasantly surprised when within a few weeks over 75,000 people were following what he was tweeting. He then discovered it was more important to talk less about himself and more about his upcoming interviews. From there, he started to leverage the Twitter platform to ask thought-provoking questions like: "I'm interviewing Colin Powell tonight. What would you like to know most about Iraq or Iran?" Here is a string of tweets from the 2008 Presidential Debate between McCain and Obama:

> . . . if they twittered they'd know how to make the words fit right? (8:17 PM Oct 15 from web)

> . . . like this . . . put it on joe the plummer, personalize it. way to go mccain (8:11 PM Oct 15 from web)

> . . . mccain plan, do you rescue everybody, even guy who paid for house he couldn't afford. even . . . flippers? (8:10 PM Oct 15 from web)

> . . . Okay, i can't dance. my mother is so ashamed, she can. (3:05 PM Oct 15 from web)

> . . . many blaming palin for Mc-palin slide in polls? is that fair? what u think? (12:43 PM Oct 15 from web)

> . . . mccain: "doesn't think i have guts to bring up bill ayers" should he? how should obama respond? this could be fun, showdown okay corral.(10:47 AM Oct 15 from web)[3]

These examples illustrate why social media is so revolutionary. Rick is able to have a relationship with 75,000 people—they feel more connected with him than they had before he started to leverage the Twitter platform. By responding to Rick's questions, they think they are helping to produce the show, which in many ways they are.

Become a Modern Day Pied Piper

Rick also started following a large percentage (roughly 32,000) of the people following him. "How can he follow so many people?" you astutely ask. He isn't actually keeping tabs on their tweets unless they relate directly to his questions. (As of this writing, there were several companies trying to develop automated systems to quickly capture responses and glean the appropriate data to be used for quick polling.) He is following these people as a courtesy. The community etiquette at the time was that if people were following you, then you should probably follow them. (They will never know if you didn't read one of their tweets!) If you don't refollow someone, then you are saying that you have something more important to say than they do, which might not be the impression you wish to convey.

The next logical progression was to get them on the show. Obviously, you can't get 75,000 firemen, carpenters, tech nerds, teachers, and the like on the show. Or can you?

So Rick and his producer started asking the 75,000 followers about their thoughts on various subjects and they put it up on the general scrolling byline. This was brilliant because it added content to the show and also encouraged Rick's 75,000 followers to watch just so that they could see if their comment made the show!

In a Socialnomic world, companies need to relinquish the total control they have had over the last few centuries and allow users, consumers, viewers, and so on to take their rightful ownership. Rick Sanchez's experiment, which turned into an overnight success, can be summed up in the following tweet from Rick's producers:

> just finished editorial meeting with my group, may have great new video today. will share more shortly. like i say, it's your show. (9:31 AM Oct 21 from web)[4]

The key line in this tweet (message sent on Twitter) being "like i say, it's your show." Credit should go to CNN for allowing Rick to continue his microblogging. Rick didn't go through any formal training on microblogging, nor did he sit through public relations and brand courses at CNN on what could be said. Rather, CNN let Rick and his producers run with it. Rick was representing CNN, but because of the nature of the technology, the brand chiefs and executives couldn't approve every sentence that Rick was issuing. They had to know that Rick was going to make some mistakes but that he would quickly adjust and move forward. CNN learned from Rick and replicated his success across all their shows and anchors, and as of May 2008 had the most followers, with close to 800,000 ahead of Britney Spears and Barack Obama, respectfully.

Everybody is Twittering, But Is Anyone Listening?

Whether Rick Sanchez, Britney Spears, or Lance Armstrong has 75,000 or 750,000 followers, they're all "A-Listers." People want to hear what they have to say. It's not because of Twitter, it's because these celebrities previously had a fan base.

Now, there will be a few new A-Listers that result simply from Twitter/microblogging. However, these will be few and far between.

So, what about the rest of us? If we have 1,500 followers, are any of them really listening? I'd argue that most are not. However, it's still a huge marketing tool, and the nobodies are now the new somebody for the following reason.

Twitter and other means of microblogging are free. If a local plumber has 1,500 followers, even if most of them aren't likely to be listening at any given moment, as long as at least one person is, that's all that matters. If that one person has a plumbing issue, the plumber now has a shot at new business, especially if the plumber acquired these followers simply by limiting his search.twitter.com query to people within a 25-mile radius. For that plumber, that one listener goes from a nobody to a somebody in a hurry.

Some salient uses of microblogging:

- Businesses following what is being said about them or their industry—Zappos, JetBlue, Comcast, and so on.
- Celebrity updates—Lance Armstrong Tweets about his collarbone.
- Real-time updates of news events, especially natural disasters.
- Niche topics, like #MSU or #UNC during March Madness.
- Individuals or companies promoting themselves.

And it's the last point that may eventually cause Twitter to become tiresome. Is Dale Carnegie rolling over in his grave because everyone on Twitter is trying to be heard, when the key to winning friends and influencing people is actually listening? Some of Twitter's popularity in the beginning was the fact that not everyone was on it, giving it effectiveness and a cool factor. When it becomes flooded with marketing messages, it loses both effectiveness and uniqueness, which may lead many users to abandon Twitter and move on.

Smithsonian Student Travel sent more than 6,000 students to Washington D.C. for the presidential inauguration. In the past it would have been difficult to get major media outlets attention. However, Twitter made it easy. NPR, MSNBC, and PBS immediately replied to Smithsonian Student Travel's tweet, expressing interest in hearing from middle school students and teachers.

However, two months after that, I typed in #JetBlue, expressing my concern that their televisions may not work on my flight. This was important to me because I selected JetBlue solely for the purpose of watching March Madness on DirectTV. Instead of hearing tweets, I heard crickets chirping. It's cool when companies and even CEOs respond in real time. This was not the case, however, in this particular instance.

In JetBlue's defense, they're somewhat victims of their own success on Twitter (Morgan Johnston does a fantastic job). People expect the best from them because they've been one of the pioneers. As a result, more people tweet and follow them and it's difficult for them to keep pace.

In another example, I tweeted an interesting article about Travelocity along with #travelocity and indicated that Travelocity was in deep trouble. Here's what responses I received:

@Travelocity: How deep of trouble?

@equalman: Pretty deep as it appears Priceline has the lead and only one or two online travel agents will survive. I love the gnome, so good luck!

@Travelocity: We like Gloria Gaynor ;)

It took me a second to get it, but then I was laughing at this witty retort. Gloria Gaynor's famous disco song is "I Will Survive."

As more people join Twitter, this type of one-to-one relationship will be difficult to maintain. Many celebrities have "ghost tweeters."

In the future, instead of getting a witty and salient reply from a CEO or well-informed employee, you'll most likely get an uninspired reply from a call center (tweet center?) in New Delhi—if you're lucky enough to get a response at all. Remember, I received no response to my #JetBlue tweet, where I was surprised and delighted by the Travelocity response.

Companies should still microblog, because the upside is still greater than the downside and it's similar to building a free prospect and user data base that you can message when appropriate.

TV Repeats Mistakes of the Music Industry

During the heyday of Napster, the music industry filed lawsuit after lawsuit about these new file-sharing technologies. While copyrights are important, energy and efforts should have been placed elsewhere. Instead of actions that disenfranchised their customer base (some of the largest numbers of downloaders and sharers were made up of music fanatics) the music industry should have been rejoicing that their distribution, production, and packaging expenses became almost nonexistent!

Music labels could sell direct to customers without the need to pay for packaging, shipping, compact discs, and so on. Some would argue that they didn't embrace the model because of copyright infringement, but the real reason they didn't embrace the model is that they didn't understand it. By the time they understood the implications of such a runaway hit, it was too late. Ironically, they had been giving away free promotional records since the 1950s to radio stations. The music houses understood back then that the more their record got played, the more their sales would increase. Somehow they lost sight of this same construct in the digital era. Television executives could also make the same errors as the record labels and find themselves standing on the outside looking in. Let's take a quick look at some disconcerting developments.

NBC Earns Fool's Gold in the 2008 Beijing Summer Olympics

The 2008 Beijing Summer Olympics were the most watched games in Olympic history. The opening ceremony was the biggest television event outside the Super Bowl, reaching 34.2 million American viewers, according to Nielsen Ratings.[5] Michael Phelps' historic swimming competitions captured the nation. The recognition and use of online tools and video by NBC is commendable for that time.

So, did NBC deserve a gold medal for their coverage? On the surface, using old measures, they reached the podium, but they were awarded only fool's gold. Here's why.

There's This Thing Called the Internet

For one of Phelps' gold medals, NBC showed the action live in every time zone except on the West Coast, which was delayed three hours. Is NBC President Dick Ebersol not aware of a thing called the Internet? NBC failed to do what others had learned long ago: beg, borrow, and make better is the way of the Web.

Too many companies—in this instance, NBC—believe their problems are unique when it comes to the Web. However, plenty of other companies have already wrestled with similar issues.

Back in June of the same year, ABC made the right decision by streaming live on the Web the Tiger Woods and Rocco Mediate's 18-hole playoff to decide the U.S. Open Championship. This was in addition to their television coverage. Company web servers cringed, and America's productivity declined in March Madness-like fashion on that Monday, June 16, but ABC and the PGA were the big winners because they captivated millions of viewers on the Web that otherwise would have been lost.

Why didn't NBC do the same thing a few months later during the 2008 Summer Olympics? Most likely because . . .

Old Metrics Are Deceiving

They were fooling themselves with old metrics. Sure, NBC was happy to show less popular events online, but not precious events like swimming and gymnastics.

Why? Most likely, NBC and their advertisers (Adidas, Samsung, Volkswagen, McDonald's, Coca-Cola, etc.) were judging themselves using old metrics, and that earned them nothing but fool's gold. They're judging success on some archaic Nielsen Television Rating system. They have the irrational fear that online viewership will cannibalize their normal ratings. Eyeball are eyeballs. They would have been better served opening up their online viewership because:

- It's more measurable.
- It has a younger audience.
- Users can't TiVo through commercials.
- Users are willing to give you valuable demographic information like name, age, gender, and so on in return for video.
- It increases—not decreases—your total viewership, which means more eyes on advertisements.

Don't Lie to Your Audience

NBC treated viewers with little regard, indicating that Dara Torres would be up in 14 minutes . . . 35 minutes later she finally swam her race. Worse, one night they indicated Phelps would be on in 32 minutes, and then when the time came, it was four minutes about his eating habits—he wasn't even swimming! Not to mention the whole computer-generated-enhancement-of-the opening-ceremony debacle. As a quick refresher, they used animation on top of what was occurring at the actual ceremony so that the viewer at home had an enhanced version of what actually was occurring live.

Dead Air Equals Missed Opportunity

They got it right showing basketball in the early morning hours (8 and 10 EST) online; however, they missed two golden opportunities.

First, there was no option to hear announcers. For events like cycling, that would have been a goldmine for fans.

Second, and much worse for their advertisers, there weren't any advertisements during downtime. So, during basketball timeouts, there was just a wide shot of the court for awkward, three-minute intervals. Why didn't they use this opportunity to give their advertisers free placement during this dead air or even have additional web-only advertisers? The technology to pull this off has been around for almost a decade (remember how Mark Cuban became a billionaire when Yahoo! purchased his broadcast.com?).

5. Google Failed

It's potentially understandable that an old-school company like NBC may get some things wrong, but Google didn't exactly turn in a world record performance either.

When lesser-known athletes burst on the scene, the search engines had a difficult time serving up relevant search results. When the United States's David Neville dove for the finish line in a gallant effort to capture the bronze in the 400-meter the search results on Google showed an actor/model by the same name, along with a company that could help you find people's phone numbers.

These poor search results were consistent for many of the athletes, so much so that Yahoo and MSN attempted to manipulate the results by hand. Google finally threw in the towel and pushed news feeds and *Wikipedia* results to the top of the listings for many of the athletes. More and more people started going straight to *Wikipedia;* Jamaican runner Usain Bolt's page was updated within seconds of him breaking the record in the 200 meter.

Also, the last-minute nature of the YouTube/NBC deal was laughable. They signed the deal only days before the Olympics started. This should have been done weeks before, it's not like YouTube was new. They were the established player in the online video market. Because Google owns YouTube, Google and NBC should've placed a sponsored listing within the Google Search results for "watch Olympics on YouTube" explaining how the deal didn't cover the United States but was only for those people living outside of the United States. There were many frustrated Americans who thought they could watch

Michael Phelps on YouTube and only discovered after several minutes of frustration that this option was only available in select countries.

That being said, NBC did many things better this time around (for instance, the Microsoft Silverlight picture quality online was an advancement at the time). However, they don't deserve a gold medal for their incorporation of online tools. NBC failed to leverage best practices in regards to combining offline and online content. A bronze, or perhaps even a silver medal, is in order.

TV Shows Viewed through the Internet

It's inevitable that all of our broadcasts will eventually be pushed through the Internet. Brand budgets that historically went to television, magazine ads, and outdoor boards are moving to digital channels for three main reasons: (1) the audience has moved there, (2) it's more cost effective, and (3) it's more trackable. What will happen?

In the short term, there will be companies that are able to take advantage of this transition. Just as online travel agent sites like Priceline, Orbitz, Expedia, and Travelocity were able to take advantage of suppliers (hotels, airlines, cruise lines, rental cars) and make a slow progression to web bookings; aggressive conduit companies will be able to deliver what the audience wants. The same holds true for Napster, Limewire, and iTunes jumping on the opportunity made available by the ineptness of the music industry to embrace digital music. At the beginning of 2008, Jeff Zucker, the boss of NBC Universal told an audience of TV executives that their biggest challenge was to ensure "that we do not end up trading analog dollars for digital pennies."[6] Zucker understood that the audience was moving online faster than advertisers were, thus leaving media companies in a position of possibly losing advertising revenue and having their inventory devalued if and when they moved online with their television content. In the fourth quarter of 2008, online advertisements in video grew 10.6 percent and went from 2 percent of advertising to 3 percent.[7]

A good example of the use of this medium was also presented during the 2008 presidential election. Candidates don't care about distribution rights or upsetting their offline sponsors. They only care about getting the word out and making it as easy on their users (in this case, potential voters) to access and consume the information. Through their respective web sites, each party streamed high-definition convention coverage around the clock. This forced CNN, MSNBC, FoxNews, and the like to do the same. The major networks didn't have time to decide if they would allow the public access—they were losing their audience to these other new distribution channels. This type of hypercompetition from unexpected places is a harbinger of the future. Who could have ever guessed that our political parties would be more advanced in terms of online video than our television networks?

The way in which we view broadcasts is also changing. In the political convention example, you had the ability to select various cameras to choose how you wanted to view the process. Specifically for the Democratic National Convention, you could have selected: (1) national broadcast angle, (2) side camera, (3) backstage, (4) camera focused on Barack Obama, (5) camera focused on Joe Biden, or (6) camera focused on Michelle Obama.

This ties back to braggadocian and preventative behaviors from Chapters One and Two. For example, if you are Michelle Obama, and you are being filmed throughout the entire convention, it's imperative you make certain that you aren't chatting away with your mom during the Speaker of the House's presentation. The upside for the viewer is that it allows for a more intimate relationship with the candidates and their families because viewers can see what they are like off camera.

NBC's *Sunday Night Football* was one of the first to introduce the idea of these various camera angles. They smartly viewed it as a way to capture online viewers, but also as a way to capture their regular television viewers who had laptops open for an enhanced viewing experience. NBC allowed the users to select various angles on the field as well as select cameras that were only following star players (like Tom Brady or Peyton Manning).

Applying this concept to content-focused shows like ABC's *The View* could prove to be a further success. Marketers would serve up different product offerings to someone who was viewing via the camera that was hyperfocused on Elisabeth Hasslebeck, versus the viewer that was focused on Whoopi Goldberg.

Adjust Shows Based on Fast-Forward Behavior

Real-time data helps dictate content: with devices like TiVo in the offline world and YouTube analytics, producers of content are able to get real-time feedback about the content of their shows. If ESPN captures the TiVo/DVR information from their *SportsCenter* telecasts, and they see that fast-forward/skip rates increase 35 percent during hockey segments, it would behoove them to possibly cut this segment down or eliminate it all together. They can make these adjustments in real time.

One entity rose quickly based on its ability to recognize the consumer's demand for online video of traditional programs and movies. The site hulu.com formally moved from private beta to product launch in March of 2008. Analysts, reporters, and bloggers panned the effort as Johnny-come-lately because there were several similar options in the marketplace (e.g., Veoh, Joost) and gave Hulu a limited chance at success because it would be weighed down with its commercially supported advertising model.

By September of 2008, Hulu was the sixth most-watched video-content provider on the Web with NielsenOnline reporting 142 million streams and 6.3 million unique monthly visitors.[8] They were able to surpass such television giants as Disney, MTV, ESPN, and CNN. Much of their success can be attributed to identifying the need for high-production-quality television shows and movies aggregated in one place on the Internet. They were so successful that in October of 2008 YouTube announced that they would start offering more full-length content and original production.

An important part of Hulu's success is the direct result of their understanding of Socialnomics. They understood that the eight minutes of advertising that was generally included in a 30-minute sitcom would not be optimal for the user or for the advertiser. So, they went out of their way to ensure their 30-minute programs averaged two minutes worth of commercials. How can 2 minutes be better than eight minutes worth of commercials for the advertiser? It was worth more because the recall was much higher.

"The notion that less is more is absolutely playing out on Hulu," Jason Kilar, the chief executive of the site, said. "This is benefiting advertisers as much as it is benefiting users."[9]

According to the Insight Express survey, advertisers saw a 22 percent increase in ad recall and a 28 percent increase in intent to purchase. This caused their advertising base to grow from 10 to 110, and clients ranged from McDonald's to BlackBerry.[10] "I've been waiting for this for 10 years," said Greg Smith, the chief operating officer of Neo@Ogilvy, an interactive agency of the Ogilvy Group.[11]

In some instances, Hulu users have the ability to select the format in which they receive the advertising. They could elect to receive it all in one big chunk—usually movie trailers—or have it spread out in the typical format. The typical format for a 30-minute TV spot starts with a 30-second upfront "brought to you by," a 30-second commercial at the midway point, and then a closing commercial. Another social piece that was pure genius was that Hulu would indicate how long the commercial would be. Users don't have the ability to fast forward through commercials, but if they know it's only a 30-second commercial break, what are the odds of them getting up from where they are watching— not likely. The user likes this sense of control, and it echoes avid Internet video-fan Mary Alison Wilshire:

> I was watching *Mike and Mike* on television at the gym, and they went to commercial break for six minutes, then came back and said they would be right back, well that was another eight minutes later. A 14-minute commercial break! Also it's maddening not knowing how long the break will be. At home, I TiVo through all the commercials, but when I watch online, I don't mind the commercials on Hulu because they are so short and they tell me when the show will be back on. In fact, my husband and I play a game trying to guess who will be the sponsor of *The Daily Show.*[12]

Mr. Kilar of Hulu couldn't agree more "We think that a modest amount of advertising is the right thing because that's going to drive atypical results for marketers."[13] A survey conducted by ABC also supported this notion—seeing that only running one advertisement during a 30-minute program generated an astounding 54 percent recall rate.[14]

The format was well conceived for the user and for the advertiser. Users are appreciative that sponsors are helping to provide them with *free* television in these types of new formats. In a survey conducted by Hulu and Insight Express, 80 percent of the viewers rated their experience on hulu.com as good to excellent.[15] Users are less tolerant of commercials on cable and satellite services because they are already paying over $100 for the service. Whereas on sites like Hulu, users are most appreciative of the sponsor, because when they hear that the program was brought to them by McDonald's, they know they owe McDonald's some gratitude for making it available online for free. This same message sounds hollow to the viewer via traditional broadcast television.

This is the same concept that television embraced back in the 1950s. However, over time they kept putting the advertiser ahead of the real client—the viewer. This marginalized the viewer experience, which in turn impaired the advertiser and eventually the broadcaster. Alarm bells should ring when the technology product winner of the year (TiVo) is a direct attempt to circumvent your service offering. Instead of fighting legal battles to stop such technology, advertisers should take the socialnomic approach of understanding that something in the chain is broken and must addressed.

Contrast this with a site like Hulu where 93 percent of respondents to the Insight Express survey (18,000 surveyed) said they felt they were receiving the right amount of advertising for the free content they were enjoying. A large percentage of the sample even expressed that there could be more advertising. An estimated 14.3 million viewed the first Tina Fey "Palin Skit" on Hulu, while only 10.2 million viewed the September 13, 2008 episode on television. Of course Hulu's numbers usually benefited from the same user viewing it more than once. The September 27, 2008 skit attracted 10.1 million views on Hulu and 7.9 million views on television.[16]

Due to the popularity, Hulu actually needed more advertising, not to compensate for lost revenue but to enhance the user experience. Similar to CNET's *Buzz Out Loud* podcast example with Best Buy, it's important for the advertising to stay as fresh as the content. You can't serve up the same ad to the same viewer 20 times. The beauty of it being pumped through the Internet is that sites and broadcasters have insight into how many times a viewer saw an ad, while historically this has been something of a guessing game at best for the television ad community.

The executives of Hulu understand that sites like theirs are just as social as a *Wikipedia,* MySpace, or Facebook. That is why they have allowed users to give commercials thumbs-up or thumbs-down ratings.

Hulu's success will contribute to moving us to a more socialnomic way of viewing our favorite video content from anywhere. As of the writing of this book, SlingCatcher has launched a new product allowing users to access their home-cable-fed programming from anywhere in the world. This complements their popular Slingbox device that allows travelers to set up a small box in their hotel rooms (or anywhere outside their homes) to be able to watch their regular programs and DVR from what is being delivered to their homes. At the time of this writing, Hulu couldn't stream shows outside of the United States, which will significantly reduce future growth in the months ahead because online video delivery is a huge benefit for those traveling internationally. Once Hulu is able to overcome this hurdle, it is likely to tap into the SlingCatcher market. Even the networks are starting to run first-time programming of their most popular shows online, and our bet is that this will move into 100 percent delivery sooner than most believe.

Hulu's success may be short lived, only time will tell; but at a minimum, they understood the customer needs of their space and forced the industry to move in a new direction. As Kevin McGurn, Hulu's Vice President of National Sales pointed out at an OMMA panel:

Hulu starts mostly with professionally produced content that already has an audience. But for other content, we use what our editors think is cool, and also what is popular on the site. They aren't always the same. We want to make video as viral as possible. If you think your friends would like a video, we want you to be able to share it. Things on the web don't have to be an instant success. In fact, they generally aren't, unless they were popular somewhere else first.[17]

Another item to consider in why TV will quickly move to Internet pipes is the sociability. If you are watching a particular game, you will be able to easily inform your social network and invite other fans to join you. You will then have the ability to comment and chat real time allowing you to be connected to the tailgate in Columbus, Ohio, even though you are sitting in San Diego, California.

The end winner here will be the consumer because these innovative tools and companies, no matter if they last or not, will bring new ideas to the table and change the way that we as consumers have been trained to accept broadcast media.

We started to see a glimpse of this in April of 2009 during CBS's broadcast of the Masters. They had online streaming of the event in high definition. It was full coverage for the first two days and then for the last two days you had your choice of four holes to watch. Again, it wasn't quite all the way there, because why wouldn't you show the entire thing? It's all about distributing your product. The more people see your product, the more people see your client's advertising. In many instances, when people are working the only option they have for watching an event is via the Internet. Also, more and more people are choosing to forgo an expensive monthly cable bill and they make do with simply their Internet connection. This should sound oddly reminiscent of a trend that happened about 10 years ago—people started to not have a landline in their house or apartment' rather they got by with their mobile phone. The same could happen in the television industry.

Most likely we can anticipate some intense legal battles in Washington, because the foreseen problem is that many of the suppliers of cable television are also the suppliers of the Internet connection!

If Time Warner or Comcast starts to see more and more people cut their $150 monthly cable television bill, they could react by increasing the fee for the Internet connection or set up pricing models to charge per stream. We can only hope that competitors and alternatives for high-speed Internet emerge or that policies are put in place to obstruct this type of malicious behavior.

Circling back to the 2009 Masters: On the final two days CBS showed only four holes. A few years from now we will be in a much better place. I would predict that not only will there be full coverage over the Internet, but that the viewer will be able to select which hole, or which player, they would like to watch. The power will be in the users' hands, which is where it should be.

Scrabulous—A Fabulous Example

A great example of what not to do involves Hasbro and two entrepreneurs from India. Quickly identifying the potential of the Facebook application platform, two young programmers in India, Rajat and Jayant Agarwalla, thought there might be interest from people playing Scrabble against each other across the globe. They couldn't find an acceptable version of Scrabble to play online so they decided to create their own. They named it "Scrabulous" as a direct reflection of the game (Scrabble) that they were adapting. Scrabulous co-creator Jayant Agarwalla indicated he sent a letter to Hasbro in January 2008 asking for permission to use the trademarked Scrabble template. He never heard back, and took that as permission to go ahead with his program.

There was more than enough interest with over 500,000 daily users at its peak. The application became one of the top-10 most-used applications on Facebook,[18] and during a 2008 interview on CBS's *60 Minutes,* Facebook founder Mark Zuckerberg even mentioned that he enjoyed playing against his grandparents. Speaking of grandparents, it was estimated that 40 percent of the players were over 50 years old, which proves what we've been saying throughout this book—social media is for everyone. Who knew that such an old game would be so enormously popular in a Web 2.0 world?

When the Agarwalla brothers eventually heard back from Hasbro, they were issued a cease-and-desist letter and a lawsuit was filed against them for copyright violation. At first glance, you could argue that Hasbro/Mattel took the logical route in protecting what they rightfully own by suing Scrabulous for copyright infringement. However, it is apparent that they may have missed the bigger picture and, better yet, the opportunity to capitalize on the existing user base who likely associated Scrabulous with the makers of Scrabble anyway. We can't help but wonder if the legal cost and negative publicity have simply washed away the potential profits that Scrabulous was *freely* providing Hasbro/Mattel. So it would seem that rather than suing the online game's creators, Hasbro could have formed a partnership with them or bought them out.

"But in today's fast-changing social networking environment, Hasbro's lawsuit and its attempt to control its online image may not be the right move," said Peter Fader, co-director of the Wharton Interactive Media Initiative. He believes Hasbro's action is an "incredibly bad business decision. " There is no evidence that the Agarwalla brothers were doing 'something absolutely disparaging' to the Scrabble brand. In fact, Scrabulous has been such a fabulously good thing for the Scrabble franchise [that] Hasbro should have been celebrating."[19]

"It is not clear if Hasbro did the right thing by going after Scrabulous," chimed Kevin Werbach, Wharton professor of legal studies and business ethics. "Many copyright owners today are over-inclusive as they try to assert their rights. The question for Hasbro is whether the benefit they get in terms of direct and indirect revenue from their own Scrabble game exceeds the cost of negative publicity from this action. But it certainly got them a black eye in the online community, although most people who play Scrabble have no idea this has happened."[20]

In the dismantling process, on the morning of July 29, users were abruptly denied access to the Scrabulous application on Facebook. If positioned correctly, Hasbro could have capitalized and made a strategic move with an introduction of their own Online Scrabble. Had Hasbro been ready to launch their internal electronic Scrabble application, the transition would have been almost seamless to the user, and Hasbro would have continued to profit from the free Scrabulous publicity. Instead, users found that the Hasbro Scrabble application was jammed with glitches, extremely slow to load, and the variety of word selection (the basis of Scrabble) was poor compared to any *Webster's* dictionary.

You could argue that those who really lost out from this debacle are both the end users, who are left with a less than optimal product, and Hasbro, who mistakenly believed that Scrabulous users would adopt their version of online Scrabble. As one avid Facebook user posted,

> You didn't have the smarts or initiative to come up with as good a product as the boys did, so your alternative is to mess with the superior product? Do you think that the thousands of folks who were enjoying this superior application will now come running to your inferior product?[21]

The numbers have proven exactly that. At the launch of Hasbro's official version of online Scrabble, the game attracted fewer than 2,000 daily Facebook users compared to the more than half a million players a day worldwide on Scrabulous. Another issue with the new application was that there were various groups holding the rights from country to country. So, for the main Scrabble game, it was no longer a global game, but only for U.S. and Canadian citizens. What a great benefit for society, millions of people connecting with others across the globe to play an educational game like Scrabble. The Agarwalla brothers may well have been on their way to a Nobel Peace Prize (admittedly a stretch) before Hasbro spoiled the fun.

According to Fader, many companies sue "just because they think they have the right to, instead of pursuing what's in their shareholders' best interests." It is "irrelevant if Hasbro was right or not" in its copyright claims against the backdrop of how Scrabble benefited from Scrabulous, he says. "The downside they have created for themselves and others is a lack of an upside."[22]

Companies "need to move aside from knee-jerk tendencies to bring in legal action," he adds, noting that Hasbro had other options besides suing. "It would have been smart to pay (the Agarwalla brothers) millions of dollars. That would have been minuscule compared to legal fees and their own application development expenses. . . . Hasbro may have won the battle but it has surely lost the war."[23]

As of the publication of this book, the Agarwalla brothers, were in the process of designing a version of chess for Facebook as well as Wordscraper, a Scrabble-like game in which players make up their own board configuration. Let's hope the originators of these games do not commit the same mistake as Hasbro. If these games grab even one-fourth of the attention that was generated by Scrabulous, the Agarwalla brothers will merely take the Hasbro experience as a stepping stone into the fortune that awaits them. It is estimated that the Scrabulous game had been generating advertising revenues in the range of $25,000 per month for the Agarwalla brothers.

If there is a lesson to be learned from all this, it would be that it is best to weigh your options (like TripAdvisor did with Cities I've Visited) before jumping in to claim what is rightfully yours. Take advantage of others who have already done the legwork to help you position your brand throughout the social media space. Think strategically before exposing your brand. Hasbro failed to anticipate the speed at which users would react to the abolition of Scrabulous and the introduction of Online Scrabble. They could have favorably capitalized on the work done by the Agarwalla brothers; but instead, they chose to fight the battle uphill. All of this translated into lost potential revenue and advertising dollars, which diminished brand equity and ultimately ignored what appears to have been in the best interest of shareholders—partnering with the Agarwalla brothers instead of launching against them in a multimillion-dollar lawsuit. Online Scrabble by Hasbro eventually did find its way back to roughly similar users as Scrabulous, but at what cost?

Advertising within Social Networks Is Actually Effective

Because social media lends itself to unobtrusive advertising, that advertising is effective. In a 2008 survey done by Razorfish—"The

Razorfish Consumer Experience Report" 76 percent of the 1,006 people surveyed said they didn't mind seeing ads when they logged-in to Facebook, MySpace, or other social media sites. Razorfish also found that 40 percent of the respondents said they made purchases after seeing those ads.[24]

Intuitively this makes sense because social media can accomplish things that we weren't necessarily able to do in the past. For example, when my friend changed her status from "In a Relationship" to engaged, she started getting ads for wedding photographers, DJs, and so on. This was information that she didn't necessarily view as advertising, but rather part of the experience—and a helpful part at that.

Smart companies like TripAdvisor understand this technique and approach the market from an outside-in viewpoint rather than from the old inside-out paradigm. ACME Travel was using inside-out thinking and old metrics. They approached the opportunity of Facebook from the perspective of "How can we grow our database so that we can mail potential customers brochures and send them e-mail?" Actually, the question that companies should ask first is "What do we have to offer that is unique and valuable to our customers and potential customer base?" Also, engaging in role-playing in which you put yourself in the shoes of your users is always extremely beneficial. As a user would I take the extra step of giving you my personal information? Only if what the company is offering is valuable enough to me that I choose to forfeit my personal information.

Users generally want to be communicated with through the medium in which you met to begin with. In this example, TripAdvisor knows that they will be communicating through the user's Facebook inbox or Facebook news feed, not via traditional e-mail or brochures. At some point during the relationship, if the user wants to sign up for an e-mail distribution, then TripAdvisor will be more than happy to accommodate them.

A few months after the travel application battle, ACME Travel was discussing a different Facebook tactic, establishing a fan page. A fan page is usually for your company or product home page within Facebook. Facebook users can select a simple "+" symbol, and they are added as fans so that they can receive updates in their news feeds for anything going on with that product or service. There was a heated debate about what adjustments they should make to the fan page prior to a large e-mail drop that was going to deploy later that week. For several weeks, ACME showcased two products on their fan page. The various product managers were arguing about which product should be placed higher on the page and how many outbound links they should have driving to lead forms. This is a classic example of a traditional marketing pitfall; people arguing for months over the color of a car to be featured in an upcoming commercial, or disputing if a URL should be printed as www.company.com or http://www.company.com in the next edition of a magazine ad. This type of behavior is nonstrategic and wastes energy because the decisions are not being driven by consumers of the product or service.

Fortunately for ACME, the new social media director sat patiently quiet while the quarreling continued and finally intervened with

> We already know what needs to go on top. Italy Vacation Packages has always been on the bottom, which is harder to see and historically this position gets less clicks. However, what we have seen is that Italy Vacation Packages has outperformed France Vacation Packages. Our data shows that more people have clicked on Italy Vacation Packages and there are 90 percent more comments and pictures posted about these packages versus the France Vacation Package. It's not for us to decide; the users have already decided for us. Italy should go to the top of the fan page. Also, we will not have any outbound links to our lead-capture forms on this main page, we don't want to make the same mistake again that we made with the application.

I was sitting in this meeting at the time, and the meeting room went silent when this was expressed. The meeting was over shortly thereafter. In the past, meetings had gone on for hours resulting in the wrong decision or even a compromise. With the advent of social media, this type of discussion ceases to exist. Business decisions become more about letting the user decide what's important. As discussed at the beginning of this section, this is commonly referred to as outside-looking-in thinking, and it is being driven by social media.

Content and Conversation Will Drive Awareness— Not Advertising

More and more companies will be developing content in the form of webisodes (five-minute episodes that could be a series), applications, and widgets. Money historically spent on media will be spent to develop and promote this varying content.

Sometimes, this content will be developed from the ground up by the companies themselves—think soap operas on steroids. A good example of this is EF Educational Tours 2009 web series "Life On Tour." It's a story of six students who go on a tour abroad. Produced by Bunim/Murray Productions, best known for their MTV "Real World" series. There is no overt marketing placement in the show itself except at the end with a small EF logo. While on the tour abroad, teenagers can chat with the cast members on their Facebook page.

Advertising will be less about social media *campaigns* and more about an ongoing conversation.

Other times, the idea or content will already have been produced, and companies will join forces, often with individuals who may go from being nobodies to somebodies overnight because of the power of the social graph.

Don't Put All Your Eggs in One Basket

How do companies know what the next great thing is? How do they avoid missing out on a great opportunity without overexposing themselves? Some argue that given the speed of technology, companies should try everything; they should throw a bunch of small tests out against the proverbial wall and see what sticks. If budgets and resources were not at the forefront of profitability, this would make sense. But with the importance of watching every dollar and companies trying to increase their return on investments, a more strategic approach should be taken. For example, if your company is about to foray into one of the big social networks, it's best to understand fundamentals as they relate to:

- **What** you are doing
- **Where you are doing it**
- **Why** you are doing it
- What **success** looks like
- What potential **pitfalls** you may encounter

The best way to look at these five pillars is through a real world example: my Mom's friends' summer cheerleading camps, one of the largest in the country.

What

My mom's friend Betsy knew that there was a need for a community centered around the camps so that the kids could interact, and Betsy decided that they needed two things in the short term: (1) A group or fan page to attract the kids, and (2) a tool or application that would allow the kids to easily connect and interact. The first few months would be a beta release. This was a wise idea that took minimal time to set up. Companies sometimes fall into the trap of trying to make everything perfect before releasing it into the wild. This harkens back to old Procter & Gamble schooling—a model that doesn't work well in social media space because it moves too slowly; the world would pass you by before you got anything out the door. If the initial setup costs make sense, it's better to get an idea out the door and run the risk of it failing than not doing anything at all.

The old paradigm of spending 14 months to produce a 30-second television commercial is counterproductive. Customers appreciate the speed at which you deliver innovative products to market and are forgiving with beta sites. Users will go out of their way to help you accelerate the release from beta to big time if they feel the product or service is worthy of the investment. Moreover, if users aren't helping you with the beta, you should be appreciative of the feedback and understand that they are advising you that there is probably not a need for you idea in the marketplace. As a company, you profit not only from releasing those ideas that your consumers have beta tested, but you also avoid costly upfront fees and development time on ideas that generate a negative return.

The head counsel indicated that they easily could have made this a six-month project by having the application pull information from a database to determine where the campers would be assigned at the start of the year. Instead, Betsy's socialnomic idea pulled the information from the campers themselves to determine where they should be assigned. The campers input data, and the application showed who was in each location based on the input rather than having it pull from a database. This is an important intention in socialnomics—*companies don't have to do everything*—users/customers are willing to help!

Where

Betsy wasn't going to have her campers come to her, rather she would go to them. She did some quick research on where most of her campers spent their time. Because they were rural and younger (14 to 16 years old), they used several social media tools, but seemed to spend a majority of their time on MySpace with some campers using Facebook. She didn't know if they would be interested in a community, but knew that her greatest chance for success would be on MySpace. If successful, she would then roll it out to Facebook and other similar avenues. She avoided a mistake that many companies fall into, trying to build every possible iteration from the get go. Betsy knew that an approach of this nature would get her nowhere.

Why

The reasons for taking this project on was to (1) keep the kids excited and engaged leading up to camp, (2) have them develop new relationships prior to the camp in an effort to reduce cancellation rates, (3) gain some potential viral exposure by having campers tell their friends about the idea, (4) establish a continued conversation with the campers to gain valuable real-time feedback, and (5) allow past campers the ability to stay connected and provide advice to first-time campers.

Success

So many times companies fail to ask themselves, "What does success look like?" It's important for companies to show a united front when it comes to their definition of success, otherwise the team responsible for implementation may be striving for something that is different from what the executives deem as important. In this example, success was going to be measured by (1) how many people joined the group and (2) determining if those who added the "meet other campers" application had a lower cancellation rate than those campers that didn't interact with the group or download the application.

Notice that success wasn't judged by how many of the campers continued their interactions or comments/postings within the application. Betsy knew that a lot of the kids would meet via the application but would then extend their relationship to other places (e-mail, phone, text, social media mail, etc.). She knew that it was analogous to introducing people at a house party and expecting that every time these people interacted it had to be at the same house where the original party was hosted.

By aggregating all of these campers into one area, the organization knew they had to watch for two key elements (1) the competition would find it easier to pick off their high schools, and (2) potential pedophiles who might descend on this collection of high school campers. The camp programmers made sure to put in the necessary safeguards to help thwart such activity without strangling growth from legitimate campers.

Pitfalls

Companies that believe in a Socialnomics world must understand and be willing to unleash control over their brands. Companies that wish to produce a 100 percent fail-safe program in terms of brand and user security are doomed to paralysis. These companies will forever remain in a development phase and miss the opportunity for execution. Companies must exercise a dosage of social responsibility, and users must also engage in best-practice behavior to ensure user security. Companies should leverage existing platforms such as Digg,

Delicious, hi5, Facebook, MySpace, and so on, which have already vetted much of the security and privacy gaps. This also shifts any potential liability to reside with the platform, not the advertiser.

In a major socioeconomic shift, individuals are taking responsibility for their own cyberactivity. This started with spam e-mails and viruses, where people quickly learned that they probably don't have an Uncle in Nigeria who has willed them $1 million. Then came the savvy and complex phisher sites. These are sites and e-mails that look like an established brand such as FedEx, eBay, or Bank of America. However, users learned to look closely at the URLs and misspellings. If the URL wasn't www.fedex.com, but something unusual like 345262.freshexample.com/fedex, then something definitely appeared *phishy*. In these examples, the major brands take painstaking steps to flush these types of scams out of the system, and in large part are reliant on their online community to alert them of such scams. However, the companies aren't responsible or liable for any loss resulting from these scams.

This isn't new to the world. If a burglar was dressed up like a Maytag repairman, Maytag is not held responsible. It is up to the person at the house to question why the Maytag repairman would be there if no repair service was ordered. Neighborhood watch programs are analogous to today's online safeguarding communities.

So when it comes to pitfalls, companies should be aware of them and attempt to mitigate them, but they shouldn't be paralyzed by them or throttle good users' abilities to get what they need from the program.

Second Life Equals Idle Life for Coca-Cola

As worldwide head of interactive marketing at Coca-Cola, [Michael] Donnelly was fascinated by its commercial potential, the way its users could wander through a computer-generated 3-D environment that mimics the mundane world of the flesh. So one day last fall, he downloaded the Second Life software, created an avatar, and set off in search of other brands like his own. American Apparel, Reebok, Scion—the big ones were easy to find, yet something felt wrong: "There was nobody else around." He teleported over to the Aloft Hotel, a virtual prototype for a real-world chain being developed by the owners of the W. It was deserted, almost creepy. "I felt like I was in *The Shining*."[25]

Donnelly and Coke went ahead and invested some serious dollars into hiring a consulting company to help them get up and running on Second Life. If it didn't feel right, then why would you go ahead and invest in it?

According to Joseph Plummer, chief research officer at the Advertising Research Foundation:

> The simple model they all grew up with—the 30-second spot, delivered through the mass reach of television—is no longer working. And there are two types of people out there: a small group that's experimenting thoughtfully, and a large group that's trying the next thing to come through the door.[26]

Another important piece in this Second Life example is to take a step back and truly assess the potential upside. It's easy to have your vision blurred by hype and propaganda. In this Second Life instance Wired Magazine points out what the opportunity really was:

> Second Life partisans claim meteoric growth, with the number of "residents," or avatars created, surpassing 7 million in June. There's no question that more and more people are trying Second Life, but that figure turns out to be wildly misleading. For starters, many people make more than one avatar. According to Linden Lab, the company behind Second Life, the number of avatars created by distinct individuals was closer to 4 million. Of those, only about 1 million had logged on in the previous 30 days (the standard measure of Internet traffic), and barely a third of that total had bothered to drop by in the previous week. Most of those who did were from Europe or Asia, leaving a little more than 100,000 Americans per week to be targeted by U.S. marketers.[27]

How do companies find the right balance between launching every possible idea through the door and ensuring they are not missing out on a great opportunity? If you have been paying attention, for success as a company in the Socialnomics world it is critical to

1. *Leverage the success that is out there.* It doesn't necessarily have to be built from within—swallow the pride pill
2. *Leverage your loyal customers.* Understand that they will help you build and adjust real time
3. *Don't overinvest.* Build light betas that can quickly be tested and adjusted
4. *Take the time to decide where you will be.* Don't try to be everywhere. Once you decide be quick and be decisive.

Worse than making a Second Life mistake is doing nothing. As someone once said "I'd rather live a life making mistakes than a life doing nothing." Even so, there are still a large number of companies that have been slow to embrace and benefit from social media.

As a company, you don't necessarily need to be the *first* to move, so don't feel like you've completely missed the boat if your company hasn't done anything to address social media. Sometimes it's prudent to sit back, and watch and learn from some of the more nimble players in the space. In social media, small businesses are sometimes the best to watch and imitate. Many of them have already waded in and learned some valuable lessons from their successes and their mistakes.

Search Engine Optimization for Facebook

Imagine if you were a mortgage lender and could go back in time to 1999 and optimize your home page for the query "Low Finance Rate." Would you do it? Of course you would. Well, the same opportunity exists today with social networks. Let's assume that the owner of Cathy's Creative Mugs (a fictitious small business) wants to post a fan page on Facebook, essentially a company promotional flyer. When prompted by the Facebook interface to name her fan page, she begins to type "Cathy's Creative Mugs," but then realizes she can probably leverage search engine optimization (SEO) best practices here. So instead, she names this page "Coffee Mugs," which is a rich keyword for her industry.

This will help Cathy return searches on "coffee mugs" within Facebook, as well as boost her rankings in the traditional search engines like Google, Yahoo, and MSN.

In many of the social media pieces, the first few years will be a "land grab of opportunity." Just like in the search world, if you were a savvy web site back in the late 1990s and ranked high for major keywords like "mortgage loans," "cheap travel," "wedding favors," and the like, you made out like a bandit. If you are one of the savvy first movers, in the first few years in social media you could set yourself up for some hefty revenue streams down the road. A good case in point is for fan pages on Facebook. There is a fan page for chocolate milk that as of April of 2009 had over 1.4 million fans! Imagine how much power the user who started that page has with Hershey's?

While as a company you can sit back and learn, you better not take too long to do it—you need to launch and learn. Companies that still think they control whether they "do" social media or not are terribly mistaken. If you're a large brand, you can rest assured that there are conversations, pages, and applications constantly being developed around your brand and by the community at large. The community is "doing" social media even if you choose not to.

John Deere Mows Over Facebook

Want proof? Let's take a look at a Web 2.0 product like a lawnmower. If you performed a search within Facebook in August of 2008 for "John Deere," you'd see:

- More than 500 groups dedicated to John Deere.
- More than 10,000 users in the top-10 groups.
- All groups were developed by the John Deere community, not John Deere corporate headquarters.
- Their chief competitor, Caterpillar, had a page in the top-10 listings.
- A group called "John Deere Sucks!!!!" is ranked in the top 10.

This is a great example, because:

- Your users will take ownership in your brand and will *do something* in social networks (both positive and negative) even if your company chooses not to.
- This has huge potential—10,000 users in the first 10 groups alone—kudos to the power of the John Deere brand.
- Your competition and your users can leverage a recognized trademark to their advantage—unless you hired a few new staff to dedicate their time to cease and desist letters.
- Malicious postings (*"John Deere Sucks!!!!"*) can show up high in the rankings if you don't have more favorable listings to push it down to insignificance.

Who has the power now: John Deere or the kid who posted the *"I love John Deere"* group? Just like in the person who started the chocolate milk page, in this instance, the kid has the power. After all, what's to stop this kid from posting a nice static image of a special offer for a competitor like Caterpillar on his site? Money talks, and this could be a cheap purchase for Caterpillar to a highly specialized target audience.

Many of these constructs are similar to SEO best practices. The person who works the smartest will win.

Sheep without a Shepherd

Another reason a company may decide to do nothing? They don't want to aggregate their hard-earned customers in a public forum because they're afraid the competition will come in and pick them off.

This might be a valid concern, as many companies crawl and scrape the Internet looking for client names of their competitors so they can poach them through various sales methods. If your fans and enemies in the social networks weren't doing anything without you, then maybe it could be a valid strategy to be safe and not aggregate your clients or fans all in one place. But, as evidenced by the John Deere example, they're out there, mobilizing around your brand, they are far from doing nothing, so you need to join the conversation. Also, if your customers are that easy to pick off, you have likely failed to build brand equity or produce a great product or service and thus probably have much bigger issues to address than your social media efforts being easily viewed by the competition The beauty of social media is that it will point out your company's flaws; the key question is how you quickly address these flaws.

Some of these concepts are difficult to grasp, but when you choose to do nothing, it's analogous to: A shepherd (company) watching over his flock of sheep (customers/users). In this analogy, a fence breaks, and the sheep suddenly have access to a new pasture (social media). More than a few wander into this new pasture because it has a lot to offer. The shepherd (company) is uncertain about what to do and decides not to go into this new pasture to find his sheep. What's most likely to occur? Sheep may get eaten by a wolf (competition), or they may get lost (customers frustrated that they can't find what they're looking for). There is no doubt that if the shepherd herds the sheep into a flock, the wolf (competition) has a better idea of where the sheep are.

However, in a flock, even though the sheep are all in one easy-to-find place, the sheep are less vulnerable, because there is safety in numbers and the wolf is less likely to attack. Also, if an attack were to occur, the shepherd will be well aware of what occurred and can better prevent it in the future. If the shepherd were to have done nothing, when the fence broke his sheep would be getting eaten by wolves, getting lost, and falling off cliffs, and he wouldn't have a clue until he went out to find them—and by then it would have been too late. Even if you decide not to herd your sheep, you should be in the new pasture helping to guide your sheep away from dangerous cliffs and waterfalls.

As a company, you need to be aware of the wolf and proactive to any reaction the wolf may have. There is no question that your competition will be out culling the Web for information that will help give them an advantage (looking for potential customer names, pricing, etc.). Transparency is definitely a two-way street. While it is great for the customer, it is also great for your competition.

As a company, you should also be out culling for information to give you an advantage. While it may win you new customers, it should also alert you to how the competition is grabbing your information. This will give you ideas on how to safeguard where you can divulge information and where the downside outweighs the benefit. As discussed in another section in this book, if your customers are that easy to pick off, then you don't have a problem with your social media or online strategy, you have a problem with your product.

1. Making multiple mistakes within social media is far better than doing nothing at all.
2. If you're a large brand, you can rest assured that there are conversations, pages, and applications constantly being developed around your brand and by the community at large. The social community is "doing" social media even if your company chooses not to.

Chapter Eight

More Winners and Losers in a 140-Character World

> I didn't have time to write you a short letter, so I wrote
> you long one instead.
> —Mark Twain

People have always found extreme value in the brevity of messages. As a result of our ability to have constant connectivity, people believe that immediate, simple, and constant communication matters. These interactions can be one-to-one or open to a broader audience.

The shelf life of conversations has been dramatically shortened. In 2000, when there were only a handful of blogs, a post or article would be commented about for a full week; its half-life would be around three to four days. Today, given the myriad blogs and the expansion of microblogging tools like Twitter and FriendFeed, the half-life of conversations has been reduced from days to minutes. At the simplest of levels, this brevity has been caused by the massive amount of information readily available.

This technology isn't always about the personal and the frivolous; it can be highly leveraged in a time of crisis like a national disaster. The wildfires of San Diego in 2007 offer a good example of this. Nate Ritter, local to San Diego at the time of the fires began twittering about what was happening from "Smoke has completely blocked out the sun" to "300,000 evacuated, to relief areas which can be found here." Realizing that it would be most effective to have as many people twittering about the fires with constant updates, Nate set up the hashtag

#sandiegofire that many others quickly picked up. This helped all thoughts and news on twitter to be organized under #sandiegofire. These tweets worked in concert with other social media tools, from users uploading videos and photos to YouTube and Flickr to Google Maps showing some of the danger zones.

Another example was when two cellular cables were vandalized in San Francisco, knocking out all forms of mobile telecommunication for AT&T users. Many customers kept abreast of updates from AT&T via Twitter #AT&T updates.

Tony Blair, the former prime minister of the United Kingdom, was asked what he found most challenging about his job throughout the span of his tenure as prime minister. He responded,

> The way in which information is exchanged so quickly has forever changed the way in which people want to consume information. They demand that things be condensed into 20-second sound bites. With complex problems, this is exceedingly difficult, but to be an effective communicator and leader you need to be able to condensed complex items down to the core and be able to do this quickly.[1]

IBM ran some popular television advertisements starting in 2005 highlighting their business services division and juxtaposing long messaging versus short. The ads generally spent the first 25 seconds showing a bombastic and often pompous consultant using big and long buzzwords in long sentences to discuss what a company should deploy as its strategy. The last five seconds usually pulled the rug out from under these suggestions with an intelligent quip, "Can we implement it?" or "How does this make us money?" to which the pompous consultant usually returned a vapid stare or scratched his head.

Karl James Buck, a graduate student at the University of California-Berkley, found out just how powerful one word can be in April of 2008. Karl was in Mahalla, covering the political unrest in Egypt. One day, things got extremely heated and some of the protestors began throwing Molotov cocktails at government buildings. Afraid they would be arrested, Buck and his translator began to retreat from the area. The police quickly halted their progress. Thinking quickly on his feet, Buck sent out a text to his Twitter network with one word "arrested." One of his colleagues was an Egyptian student studying abroad at Berkley. She along with several others who received the text immediately became worried and set themselves in action, contacting local Egyptian authorities and having UC-Berkley hire local legal counsel.

"The most important thing on my mind was to let someone know where we were so that there would be some record of it . . . so we couldn't [disappear]," Buck said. "As long as someone knew where we were, I felt like they couldn't do their worst [to us] because someone, at some point, would be checking in on them."[2] Twitter co-founder Biz Stone knew that this type of platform could be used for larger-purpose items because they had previously tested the technology during earthquakes in the San Francisco area. "James' case is particularly compelling to us because of the simplicity of his message—one word, 'arrested'—and the speed with which the whole scene played out," Stone said. "It highlights the simplicity and value of a real-time communication network that follows you wherever you go."[3]

Power to the People

If power is being transferred more and more to the people via social media mechanisms, what other forms does this take and look like? First, anytime there is a macroshift, a small window of opportunity is unlocked where companies and people can benefit. Most evident are the neophyte companies of the dot-com boom who received good money from venture capitalists. You saw companies go from a garage to multimillion-dollar corporations overnight. You also saw people win. At one point, a company called "All-Advantage" was paying people by the hour so that a bar beneath their browser could scroll ads, and working like the Amway model, if you were able to get more people to use the advertising scroll bar, you received a commission for their viewing as well. Some people were making thousands of dollars per month just to surf the Web. Others were ordering their groceries online and having them delivered by a company called Web Van. In the gro-

cery store and at gas stations, some people were paying one-fourth of
the normal price because the price was set on Priceline. Eventually
many of these ideas failed or were modified. It's not likely we will see
such an overt shift with the explosion of social media. In fact, this evolution of the Internet will probably mirror the shift we saw with the
preeminence of search. Not quite as flashy and obvious, but certainly
more powerful in shaping how we behave, live, and work.

In theory, the idea that All-Advantage embraced was noteworthy—
paying consumers for the placement space rather than going through a
middleman (buying outdoor boards, interactive banner placement on
highly visited sites, etc.). However, All-Advantage failed miserably at
execution. All-Advantage was serving ads based on what the user
selected they were interested in, but they neglected to understand that
a user's mere interest does not translate into purchases and so the
placement of the advertising alone was not sufficient to justify the
spend.

The construct was sound, but the world and technology available
just weren't ready for it. The world will be more than ready in the next
few years. We will see more than a few business models constructed
to take advantage of this shift, and only time will tell what the best
model is, but it's interesting to see some already taking shape.

Customers Get Paid for Their Search Efforts

One shift we will see is that the money previously dispersed to
middlemen is now being redistributed to the companies themselves
and to the consumers. It is given to consumers through lower-priced
products and services and most often through referrals and incentive
payouts. A good example of what some programs will resemble is
Microsoft's Live Cashback program. In 2008, Microsoft announced
it would be giving cash back to people who use Live Search (i.e.,
search at msn.com) and subsequently click-through and make a purchase.

This program is vaguely analogous to the credit card cash back programs; search engines that give cash back. By the time this book is
published, MSN's program could be defunct for several reasons. Or, it

could be a wild success. That's not the point. What we want to high-light is that these are the types of programs that we will see in a social-nomics world.

For Those Who Think This Will Never Work . . . Surprise, It Already Does

People often mistake anything on the Web as new, when in fact the construct is often not new at all. It is only the delivery mechanism that's new and innovative. Microsoft giving cash back for searches is very similar to a frequent flier/hotel stay program. Let's look at an example:

> Starwood has many hotel properties (W, Sheraton, Westin, etc.) = Microsoft's 700 merchants
>
> Users call Starwood reservations = Users search on MSN Live
>
> Starwood gives points for bookings = Microsoft gives cash back for purchases/bookings

What Model Does This Hope to Replace?

This type of model is geared toward augmenting and ultimately replacing the existing paid-search model. The historic paid-search model consisted of:

- Advertiser spends money based on an anticipated return on investment
- Search agency is typically paid a percentage of the buy
- Search engine is paid a cost per click based on an auction
- Resulting in the searcher receiving no payment, even though they driving all the revenue stream

As you can see from this model, there are two points where the majority of the money is flowing to middlemen. A percent is going to the search agency and a percent is going to the search engine. Now let's take a look a potential socialnomic model. Keep in mind that this is a similar model to *MSNBC*'s *Live* Search cashback program intro-duced in 2008:

- Advertiser spends money based on actual return—a sale is completed
- Search engine receives a percentage of revenue derived
- Searcher receives a discount or cash back

The winners and losers in this new model can be strikingly obvious. The consumer is the big winner because he or she is now getting a cheaper product as a result of less wasted money in the middle. Another winner is the advertiser who is spending less to acquire a consumer or purchase, and there is less risk associated with the transaction. In the historic model, the advertisers were paying based on a cost per click in the hope that the click would lead to an action (i.e., purchase of a good or service, subscription, lead). In the socialnomic model, advertisers are only paying per action (cost per action). Another winner of this model is the search engine that deploys it most effectively in an effort to gain market share. Coincidently, the search engine incumbent (e.g., Google) would be the least likely to introduce such a model. By endorsing such a shift, Google could see itself as a potential loser because it currently generates a fair amount of money from the inefficiency of the old model.

Because the search engines are paid on a per-click basis, if a customer found exactly what he or she wanted on the first try and were ready to purchase, this would diminish the revenue because the transaction would be completed with just one click. Whereas if it takes 20 clicks to get that one purchase, the search engines' revenues are 20 times greater.

The most obvious loser in this potential model is the search engine agency. If search engines are able to handle the entire transaction, and they have a vested interest to produce a sale versus a click thru, and this is performed efficiently, then the middleman (agency) ceases to add value in the chain and so, ceases to exist. The key and critical piece here is the ability for the search engine to optimize both its best interest and the advertiser's—which should be the same.

Let's take a quick look at this example using vacuum cleaner manufacturer, Hoover::

Historic Search Model

- *Advertiser:* Hoover is willing to pay $50 to produce a sale for their $200 vacuum cleaner.
- *Search engine:* Hoover has determined that it takes roughly 15 clicks to produce a sale and therefore is willing to pay the search engine $3 per click (3 x $15) = $45.
- *Search agency:* The search engine agency charges 11 percent commission; resulting in $5 for this buy going to the search engine.
- *Searcher:* Must pay $200 to purchase the vacuum cleaner.

Socialnomic Model

- *Advertiser:* Hoover is willing to pay $50 to produce a sale for their $200 vacuum cleaner. In the historic model, they paid $50, but in the socialnomic model they will pay a net of $40.
- *Search engine:* Hoover has agreed to pay the search engine 10 percent commission of total revenue produced. So in this instance, the search engine will receive $20 for the sale.
- *Search agency:* $0 because they are no longer part of the process.
- *Searcher:* Receives $20 cash back if they purchase the vacuum cleaner; net cost ($200 – $20) = $180.

Once the socialnomic model is multiplied by a larger revenue stream, the gains are enormous.

So you ask, why on earth would a search engine do this? The non-marketing leading engine (e.g., *MSNBC Live* Search cashback) would do so to help differentiate themselves by perfecting this model in the hopes of capturing more marketing share and in turn more revenue. Competition in the market space breeds innovative ideas that ultimately benefit the end user. In the search engine space, the "it's an auction model" argument doesn't fly as this example clearly points out. If there is a monopoly in the search engines, the consumer and manufacturer both lose. However, in the previous socialnomic example,

Hoover paid less ($40 instead of $50) and the consumer paid less ($180 instead of $200).

Join Them before They Beat You

Media giant Viacom offers a good example of a company realizing it is better to embrace social media rather than fight it (like the music industry did to music sharing). Viacom was aggressively trying to impose a "no" strategy from the beginning. They were suing YouTube for upwards of $1 billion for allowing users to post copyrighted content through its service. Originally Viacom's strategy was "Let's sue YouTube and block this." However, they quickly realized that would not work. Instead, now the solution is "Let's create a system where content can derive some benefit,"[4] said Forrester Research analyst James McQuivey.

The courts determined that YouTube wasn't responsible for proactively policing content; rather, they were responsible for removing content if the appropriate paperwork/complaint was filed by the copyright owner (e.g., Viacom). This was obviously a somewhat laborious process for YouTube to constantly strip its site of content. Also, it wasn't good for the user, because it meant there was less of the content that the user desired. At the same time, it wasn't good for the copyright owner of the material either because they had to go through the tedious process of finding the violation and then submitting the request through the proper channels to have the content taken down.

YouTube at this point in time had yet to produce a profitable return for its parent company Google. Realizing that the current "fighting" model wasn't working well for anybody, YouTube came up with a progressive solution. When they received a takedown notice, they gave the copyright owner two options: (1) remove the content or (2) keep the content up but allow YouTube to serve advertising and share in the revenue. YouTube foresaw that if they continued down the path they were on, they'd collectively be beaten. As a result, they employed the strategy of joining them (copyright owners) to their cause.

After this creative idea from YouTube, Viacom the owner of Paramount Pictures and MTV networks decided to take a similar approach with MySpace. One of the more popular activities that MySpace users engage in is passing around video content—often copyrighted video content. MySpace was more than happy to engage in a win-win relationship with Viacom. "Consumers get to share some of the content they want without having it blocked or removed," said Jeff Berman, MySpace's president of sales and marketing at the time. "This is a game changer. It takes us from a world of 'no' to a world of 'yes,' where the audience gets to curate content, express and share it as they choose, while copyright holders are not only respected, they get to make money."[5]

Contrasting this, Warner pulled all of its royalty content off of YouTube in a disagreement about how much revenue it should receive from YouTube. Time will tell if this is a poor decision. The odds are it will result in failure because the philosophy of "this is my ball so only I'm going to play with it" has failed time and time again on the Internet.

History repeats itself because no one listens the first time. This can truly be said about the strategy the Associated Press (AP) employed in April 2009. If you recall in our Jane the Blogger example, some newspapers and traditional writers have had to adapt to these rapidly changing times. Some succeed, while others fail. The AP became fixated on others failing around them and panic is the appropriate word to describe what they did next. They went with a "these are my toys and you can't play with them" strategy. This only works if you are the only game in town, which is a rare position to be in. From our Jane the Blogger story and supporting documentation, you can see that the AP is not the only game in town. But what did they do? They requested that Google remove their stories from the Google News feed. Now, legally, Google would have been fine saying your request is unreasonable, but they didn't. Google did say your request is unreasonable, but we will remove it if you desire. Sometimes it's best to take technology out of the question.

This is analogous to a record label in the 1950s asking the world's largest provider of jukeboxes to not put their songs on the juke box. A hypothetical conversation would go like this:

Juke Box Company: We could remove your songs, but then people will not be able to find them to listen to them.

Record Label: That's okay—we don't really see any direct revenue from the quarters they put into your machine, so why should users be able to listen to our music?

Juke Box Company: At that moment in time it's the only place they can listen to the song. Even if they own the record, they aren't going to carry their stereo into the bar or dance club. Don't you want people to be exposed to your music and if they like it they will come in and buy the record?

Record Label: No, these are my toys and you can't play with them.

This is precisely what the AP is doing by asking Google and YouTube to remove its content. While companies that get it are paying millions in pay-per-click and search engine optimization to rank high in Google, the AP doesn't want this free traffic and exposure. The even bigger kicker is that there was a deal in place where Google was providing some revenue share to the AP. One YouTube "so pathetic that it's funny" story went something like this:

AP: You need to pull down that YouTube AP video from your site.

AP Affiliate/Partner: No, we are an affiliate, a partner of the AP.

AP: It doesn't matter, affiliate, partner, or not, you need to remove that video from your web site.

AP Affiliate/Partner: But we pulled this off of YouTube.

AP: Even more reason to pull it down.

AP Affiliate/Partner: Yes, but you, the AP, are the ones that posted this to YouTube and supplied the imbed code that allows others to copy and play it on their respective sites. That is what we did. If you, the AP, didn't want to share this video, then why did you post to YouTube and supply the imbed code?

AP: Let me get back to you on this, but in the meantime take the video down from your site.

Panic, panic, panic is happening all around us. Companies that keep a level head will be fine and in some instances better off as their competition self-implodes.

Despite the controversial bailouts of 2008, on the technology front government and politicians are not likely to bail out companies that do not implement swift strategies to survive, nor are they willing to step into this sticky mess. President Obama's stance on this was intentionally vague. Following his election, he stated, "we need to update and reform our copyright and patent systems to promote civic discourse, innovation, and investment while ensuring that intellectual property owners are fairly treated."[6]

This is a big step for companies like Viacom; they recognize that they need to embrace social media rather than fight it. One important step to understanding this is realizing that for many large traditional companies revenue streams will be reduced, but so will costs. A prime example is on the music side, instead of $5 for a 45 record you receive $.99; you no longer are paying costs to produce, ship, and promote a physical product. However, with increased competition, it will give you the best chance to make the most money in this new space. If you resist embracing the change, you could quickly find yourself in the same declining mode currently being experienced by newspapers, broadcast news, and the music industry that failed to embrace and understand the socialnomic way of doing business. Because isn't it better to have a smaller piece of the pie than no pie at all?

Role of Search

Google product guru Marissa Mayer told the *New York Times* that social search will be a key component in the future of search. Socialommerce deserves Google's unbridled attention.

Why is Google and other search engines interested in social networks? Because, social networks are most likely to become the first place people go to perform their searches. This is already evidenced by social media site YouTube.

YouTube, which for years has been struggling to turn a profit, despite being acquired by web darling Google, eventually decided to take a play out of its parent company's playbook, and in mid-November of 2008 deployed its own pay-per-click search program. This was launched only a few days after it became the second most-searched site on the Web, dethroning Yahoo from that perch. Yes, YouTube in 2008 became the world's second-most-searched site.

It seems logical for YouTube to introduce a Google AdWords (brand name for Google's Sponsored Ad Listings)-like model so that amateur and professional videographers can easily monetize their creative materials. The model is simple, a person who uploads a video has the ability to easily place advertising that complements or is entrenched in the video. The difficulty is pairing up the advertisers to appropriate video content. For example, companies like Lexus or Puma would not want to damage their respective brands by being associated with less than top-notch creative videos. This is less of a concern in the Google AdWords model, which is text based; however, they too were able to work out the kinks several years ago when they ran into issues like an ad being served for Aflac Insurance next to an article discussing a major lawsuit against Aflac. Google worked out the kinks there, and they will work out the kinks here as well.

The truly great companies in this model are those that go beyond simply appending advertisements to existing videos. The truly great and innovative marketing minds will roll up their sleeves and get "on the ground" by being nimble and identifying quick wins and reacting adroitly when it comes to developing original content that can be a pre-roll to the video. For example, during the 2008 U.S. presidential election, when the Tina Fey "Palin" spots were popular, a brand like Budweiser could have done the preroll and said "if there was a Joe Sixpack drinking game for every time the word maverick was mentioned, you better believe the people playing it would be drinking a Bud." This played off the fact that Tina Fey was spoofing Palin for always saying Joe Sixpack and Maverick. Again this is all about becoming part of the content and enhancing the user experience rather than an interruption model. Dodge did this well in the popular NBC show *The Office* when they asked the audience during the commercial break what the bumper sticker on Dwight's desk said. This is the type of real-time stuff that engages the audience; it's part of the content rather than an interruption to it. Green Mountain coffee also ran a clever outdoor advertising campaign that was along the lines of "complete this sentence and your response could soon appear here: I'd rather be drinking a coffee…." and they supplied the number to text your response. In Chicago, Mini-Cooper billboards were reading chips in Mini-Cooper cars and welcoming the driver by name. Hello Cindy, welcome to downtown Chicago.

Originally designed for the visually impaired, the new system of tagging videos (using text to define what's in the video) makes things easy because there are tools that convert web pages into audio descriptions of the page content. These tags make it simple to categorize the Web by efficiently determining what the video content contains. Also, part of being successful in the socialnomic world, as we have discussed, is for companies to be more open and comfortable in letting go of the ownership and control of their brand. It's not going to be perfect every time, and the end user is smart—they understand that user generated content is beyond a brand's control. If 90 percent is good and only 10 percent is negative, the positive will overwhelm the negative, and the 10 percent will not cripple your brand reputation. That is a much different philosophy from the past where even the slightest negative news could destroy your brand. Heck, if there isn't 5 to 10 percent negative noise around your brand, then your brand is either irrelevant or not being aggressive enough in the space. The quickest death in this new socialnomic world is deliberating rather than doing. Fear of failure is crippling in the world of socialnomics.

This is a monumental difference in mindset compared to when well-established brands had to be almost 100 percent on message all the time—and rightfully so because it would damage the brand if something was off (e.g., Rolex sponsoring NASCAR). This could still damage a brand today, and steps should be taken to quickly resolve issues when they occur, but if you are producing a ton of noise, or more important, your consumers are producing a ton of noise around your brand, then the few blips along the way will often be drowned out by the rest.

What Happens when the Internet Advertising Structure Collapses?

The foundation for Internet advertising revenue is inherently flawed from a sustainability standpoint. Just as TiVo and digital video recorders were invented to help users avoid having to view advertising on television; tools such as pop-up blockers, spam filters, and banner blockers perform similar functions for Internet users. These Internet tools aren't limited to simply blocking only nefarious advertising activity. People also have a desire to be shielded from legitimate, but highly intrusive Fortune 500 marketing. Why? For the simple reason that these advertisers still "push" messaging rather than develop conversations with their users.

In the late 1990s, the hot dot-com start-ups weren't based on advertising revenue models; rather, they were based primarily on e-commerce models, developing steady revenue via transactions. These types of start-ups were the darlings of venture capitalists, and they shied away from start-ups that based their revenue solely on advertising models. Then during the Web 2.0 era (starting in 2006), advertising revenue models became all the rage thanks largely to the success of Google.

If you had eyes—even if you couldn't develop direct advertising relationships (e.g., advertisers pay you to have their marketing materials on your site), you could always have a fail-safe by putting Google search results on your page. This was accomplished via Google's successful AdWords program. The program allows a website owner to place contextual search results from Google on any page, resulting in instant revenue creation. Google serves up ads on a web site for example www.american-novel.com. The ads are related to the site's content. So, for this example to work, the contextual search ads placed on the pages of www.american-novel.com would be related to American authors and American novels. The owners of www.american-novel.com would be paid by Google every time someone clicked on the text ads. For example, if the cost per click for the ad was $4, Google generally would give $2 of this revenue to the owners of www.american-novel.com and put $2 into their own pocket.

This is obviously great for small web sites. It also works well for paying advertisers because they are able to generate more reach outside of just being on www.google.com. This is also good for Google because it increases their revenue stream (as of January 2009 the AdWords program accounted for roughly 10 percent of Google's revenue).[7]

However, what has been seen over time with sophisticated advertisers and robust tracking tools is that the quality of clicks coming from the AdWords network is much lower than those coming from www.google.com. The clicks weren't resulting in leads or sales.

The AdWords program is still a valuable one, but it will continue on a much smaller scale, and Google has already developed tools to allow advertisers to have more control over which sites the ads are placed on rather than placing the ads on every site in the network. For example, Nike may see that their ads don't perform well on www.american-novel.com and can remove the ads from being served there. While this type of targeting and new tools are good for the advertisers, if Google's revenue from this program dips from 10 percent (current) to 5 percent that would be significant as it would equate to over $1 billion in revenue being removed from the Internet advertising market. So many companies are dependent on Google's sustained success, for example, the open-source Firefox browser revenues in 2007 were $75 million, with search-related royalties from Google accounting for 88 percent of the total, or $66 million.[8]

Where Have All the Banners Gone?

Does online banner or display advertising get a bad rap? Yes and no. Is banner advertising going away any time soon? No. Will it be reduced? Yes. Just like a quarterback on a football team, banner advertising historically was getting too much credit when things were good and too much blame when things went bad. Because online banners were more trackable than offline marketing methods like television, radio, outdoor, and so on, they were getting too much of the credit simply from the result that they could track something. The biggest ruse was the "view-through" sale. Tracking is available to place a *cookie* (invisible pixel image) on people's web browser when they surf the Internet. If a user went to the home page of cnn.com, tracking tools would be able to see that this occurred.

When an advertiser, say 1-800-flowers, was running a banner ad on the home page of cnn.com they'd be able to see that a certain amount of users had that banner on their screen when they were at CNN. Advertisers did, and sometimes still do, make the assumption that the user saw that banner ad. Which, in some cases they probably did, in others, probably not. The second assumption that advertisers make is that if that same user takes a positive action (buys flowers or gives 1-800-flowers his information), then the advertiser gives credit to the banner for driving that action. In some cases, that is true, but in many cases, it is not. If the banner ads are the only marketing that 1-800-flowers is running at the time, they can safely assume that the action is a result of the banner campaign.

But, large companies are always running multiple advertising programs so the "clean" scenario was/is highly unlikely to ever be a reality. In reality, what occurred was that online marketers took credit for sales that may have been driven by other marketing efforts like television, radio, magazines, and so on because the online marketer had the power of robust tracking. Also this tracking cookie was set for 30 days, so if a user (Will) was on cnn.com and potentially *viewed* the 1-800-flowers banner—again there was no confirmation that Will actually saw it—just that it was on the page when he visited CNN. If Will were to buy flowers in the next 30 days, then that banner marketing would get credit for the sale when in fact it was a magazine ad that drove Will to make the flower purchase.

Marketers became addicted to this perceived success, which led to them to buying banners on millions of low quality pages at very cheap prices and having banners served to millions and millions of people. The odds of someone running across a site in 30 days that didn't place a 1-800-flowers banner cookie "on them" was very unlikely.

The primary culprits of this were the advertisers and advertising agencies. Essentially three things were occurring:

1. It never dawned on the people managing the campaign that they may be overinflating the effectiveness of their online banner marketing efforts.
2. The managing advertising agency wanted to show the best return to the client and essentially "snowballed" the client with this type of measurement.
3. The client wanted to show the best return to his executives and "snowballed" the executives with this type of tracking to garner more budget for his or her fiefdom.

We point out these items because too many companies believe that they can have a profitable and healthy online business by simply using the old advertising revenue model. This is not the case anymore. New forms of advertising online need to emerge to offset the ones that are currently broken. America Online (AOL) is a great example of this. When they decided to get out of the business of supplying dial-up and high-speed Internet connections, they figured they could merely survive with an ad revenue model—this hasn't worked out so well. Banners and display advertising will still have its place and serve a purpose, but it will be in a much smaller capacity.

Banners and display advertising will also have a place in social media, but it will be much different from the traditional banner approach. One of the huge advantages of social media for advertisers is that social networks can give them insight into a user's demographic (age, geography, occupation, etc.) and psychographic information (hobbies, clubs, networks, desires). In the past, advertisers often had to guess at this type of data. With social media, the user tells you exactly what they have been trying to determine for years. As people change, the message can change to match their lifestyle. For example in Facebook if you change your relationship status from "in a relationship" to "engaged," you will start to see relevant advertisements showing photographers, stationery options, and music providers. A few weeks later, if you make an online purchase of stationery, then these types of advertisements to you would be greatly reduced, if not completely removed. Also, some banners reflect "social actions" of those in your network. So a company placing a banner to sell lipstick can elect to have a social network to create an ad based on people's behavior around their product. So if Kelly is friends with Beth and Beth purchases the lipstick, Kelly will be served a banner with Beth's picture stating "Beth has just purchased this cherry lipstick" and probably has a picture of Beth. his banners reflecting "social actions" will be more effective than a generic banner and is one of the powers and progressive nature of social media.

However in the general Internet, we have already seen a rapid decrease in the percentage of revenue derived from display and banner advertising. In 2008, the Interactive Advertising Bureau (IAB) reported that search had overtaken display advertising, accounting for 41 percent of the market whereas display accounted for 34 percent.[9] This is radically different from 2001 when banner advertising almost accounted for 100 percent of the advertising revenue. Could we see the same type of shift from search to social media? Most likely; in Q4 2008, PubMatic indicated that the effective price that advertisers were willing to pay for display/banner ads fell 21 percent on average from the second to the third quarter, with the biggest declines coming at small and medium sites.[10]

A shift or other form of change needs to occur in order to replace such lost advertising revenue at the macrolevel. If it is not filled, the user will suffer because content companies will vanish and the free content that users have grown accustomed to will be limited or cease to exist. If a new or revised online revenue model is not found to replace this "hole," it could have a dramatic effect on the online community and on our economy as a whole. The good news is that there is a ready willingness and desire by companies to advertise on Social Media. For example 75 of the countries top-100 advertisers placed ads on Facebook in 2008 according to the company.[11]

Search Engine Results Are Still Prehistoric

Users and advertisers collectively crave more real-time relevancy from search engines. Unfortunately, due to the complexity of crawling the Web, that's inherently difficult to achieve in organic results. Why though, has it taken so long to correct this problem on sponsored search sections?

Why can't an advertiser easily alert users of a winter sale? Search engines are racing furiously to address this shortfall. The first search engine that does so will have a distinct advantage with users and advertisers. Let's look at an example.

Paid Search Relevancy Dilemma

An online travel agency sells hotels, airfare, car rentals, cruises, and so on. Because their business is centered on fulfilling demand, they're spending millions annually on search.

It's tough enough for consumers to differentiate the brands of Priceline (William Shatner), Travelocity (Roaming Gnome), and Expedia (Suitcase) in the marketplace. It's even tougher within search engines. A good example: perform a search for "Chicago Hotels." There will be 10 sponsored results showing at the top of the page and on the right rail. All the ads are almost identical. They all say "cheap hotels," "best rates," "Chicago Hotels," and so on. None of them stand out for the user. Wouldn't it be better for the user and the advertiser if the results were more specific? For example, here's a better ad:

Boutique 5-Star Hotel
- $89: Normally $299
- Next to Wrigley Building

The results are infinitely more relevant for the user. In turn, it would produce a greater return for the advertiser. So it's a win-win strategy.

How much greater is the return on investment? We tested this exact scenario within a top-10 travel company that spends around $15 million annually on search. When specific travel deals were dynamically inserted, the click-thru rate was *five times greater* than the campaign average. And, conversions were a whopping 413 percent higher.

If the returns are so great, why isn't everyone doing this? That's where it gets complex.

Tedious, Manual Feeds

Despite what Google will tell you, there isn't a simple way to set up a feed from your database that updates product pricing, specials, sales, and so on. Even if you did, you'd run into the problem of automatically generating copy that makes sense. Imagine the opportunity for a search engine that could solve this issue for Target, Foot Locker, Expedia, Home Depot, and so on.

There Must Be New Keywords

Even if you decide to hire cheap labor to upload your sales, travel deals, and so on into the search engines weekly, you'll run into an issue.

Example: Orbitz has a travel deal that is only good for the next week—50 percent off a hotel in Paris. Let's say Orbitz is buying over 100,000 keywords in their campaign. The odds of Orbitz not already buying a relevant travel keyword (e.g., Paris Hotel, Cheap Hotel in Paris) are slim.

Their campaign keywords are relevant and have built up a history over time. Due to Google's quality score, which essentially gives keywords in a campaign a good reputation over time, you can't quickly infuse new copy into Google's AdWords program. Your incumbent/generic copy that's been running the past several months will almost always win in the short term. Your new copy will have a tough time even being served in the coming week, and if it is, the cost per click is much greater.

Not giving up, Orbitz decides they'll pause all the other copy iterations for "Paris Hotel" and serve the new sale copy announcing 50 percent off. The problem here: no beneficial quality score. Orbitz would be paying more per click and would lose all the efficiencies gained. There is no easy way for them to quickly get a sale for a major city listed in search engines that makes sense from a return-on-investment standpoint.

Integration with Third-Party Optimization Tools

We haven't mentioned the complexity of an optimization/bidding tool (most likely via a third-party search agency) that Orbitz is probably employing. Many of the most popular tools in the marketplace today can't react effectively when given a short window of opportunity (less than a week) to make adjustments to existing terms within a current campaign.

Everybody loses: the user (results don't show sale), search engines (lost potential click revenue), agency (disgruntled client and lost commission), and advertiser (lost leads/sales revenue).

All of these needs seem relatively basic, at least conceptually. Will someone seize the opportunity to fill this obvious void?

Just think, we haven't even mentioned branded images and video within the search results. So, as you can see, we'll soon be looking back at search shaking our heads asking, "How did we ever survive with such a basic model?"

This is where social media will force the hyperacceleration of better search results. One size doesn't fit all. One person who searches for "Paris" may want to know about the capital of France, while another person wants to see photos of the hotel chain heiress. Also, people want to quickly type in semantic queries like "best pizza parlors in downtown Manhattan Beach, California" to get quick results from a Zagats, as well as qualitative results from their social network—this is where things will progress rapidly.

Oral Communication Skills Decline

If you don't still don't believe that some traditional interpersonal communication skills may be suffering, then maybe this example will make you a believer. Second Life is a virtual reality application that many users engage in. It's a digitized life in which you can do anything that you could in normal life. People develop avatars (digital graphic representations of themselves) sometimes reflecting who they are in real life and other times taking on different personas (a librarian may become a dominatrix). In 2008, a couple got divorced over Second Life, and here is how their story goes: Amy Taylor (28) met David Pollard (40) in Second Life, or their avatars meet each other in Second Life. Things went swimmingly, but Amy being cautious hired a

Second Life Private Investigator (yes they exist!). This investigator posed as a voluptuous virtual prostitute and tempted David inside Second Life. David resisted the temptation and passed the test with flying colors (a test he was unaware of at the time). Their courtship continued until their marriage. Because they had met in Second Life, they had their marriage ceremony on Second Life (hey, if nothing else it saved a bunch of money). Offline they signed the legal documents, and they were officially married. Things were going fine until Amy discovered that David was chatting with another female avatar (not her) and showing genuine affection. Amy was so disgusted with this that she filed for divorce both in Second Life and in the real world.

Is the Journalistic Interview Dead?

More and more interviews will be conducted on video because the cost to entry is much lower. Anyone can get a Flip/handheld camera for under $125 and have the ability to post on social media within minutes. What also has changed is the traditional "paper and pencil" journalism. For articles that will appear in newspapers, magazines, blogs, or online media, the way in which these interviews are conducted has radically changed. In the past, interviews were mostly conducted in person or occasionally on the phone. Now, they are generally conducted by the reporter or writer sending a list of questions to the interviewee. The interviewee texts, e-mails, or instant messages back their responses. This may seem inherently lazy on the part of the interviewers, but it makes sense on many fronts. It (1) allows the reporter or interviewee to save travel time, (2) saves on the hassle of scheduling a physical time, (3) saves the interviewee prep time, (4) gives the reporter a written record, (5) allows the interviewee to not misspeak, and (6) offers less chance for the reporter to misreport.

Obviously the three major downsides to this style are (1) there is no face-to-face interaction, another highlight on why people's interpersonal communication skills are diminishing, (2) the reporter may miss out on some good information that the interviewee may divulge, and (3) there is no chance for the reporter to read body language cues to determine where they've hit a spot and where they can probe further.

Mobile Me

According to a study by e-mail marketing firm ExactTarget and the Ball State University Center for Media Design, 77 percent of Internet and mobile phone users ages 15 to 17 use instant messaging, 76 percent use social networking sites and 70 percent communicate via text messaging.[12]

One of the more popular Apple iPhone applications is called "Tracker," but it could have just as easily been called Stalker. This works on the GPS in the phone to locate your friends and tell you exactly where they are. This is similar to Harry Potter's marauder's map. I guess you just need to make sure that this isn't enabled if you are trying to throw a surprise birthday party for someone. This application is also very practical for parents of teenagers—keeping track of where their kids are. "I used it on my oldest teenage daughter as somewhat of a bribe. I will get you an iPhone but on the condition that you have this Tracker application installed,"[13] said Todd Young (37) of Austin, Texas.

Opera Software shows mobile phone Internet access exploding, indicating that during 2008 use of its Min Browser on mobile phones more than tripled—reaching 5 billion page views in October. Opera said, "In many of the Southeast Asian countries the mobile Web exists not because it complements existing means of access, but rather because it replaces them,"[14] Opera added. In the United States, research conducted by The Kelsey Group and ConStat showed that 9.6 percent of mobile users were connecting to a social network as of October 2008, compared to 3.4 percent in September 2007.[15] By 2012, eMarketer projects that more than 800 million users worldwide will participate in social networks via their mobile device, up from 82 million in 2007.[16]

Field of Nightmares: Lufthansa and American Airlines

Lufthansa's statement about genflylounge.com: "GenFlyLounge is the new social networking site for Generation Fly and allows you to connect with like-minded travelers. Get the inside information from other travelers you can trust and who share your interests and travel preferences. Explore destinations before your go there. Review, add and rate tips. Join now for free!"[17]

While you can applaud Lufthansa for attempting to reach out to the next generation, you could argue that we already have too many social networks, and that we don't need another one. Lufthansa and others would be better served developing applications that work with the various forms of social media. It's that age-old cliché, "fish where the fish are." That is why I affectionately refer to it as the "Field of Nightmares." This is taking creative liberty with the line delivered by James Earl Jones postulating in the movie *Field of Dreams*: "Build it (baseball field) and they will come." In this instance, *Field of Nightmares*, you may build it and they won't come. When companies like Lufthansa decide to build an application/tool/widget that complements social media, the first question they should ask themselves is "What do we have the ability to develop that is not a poor replication of an existing tool, but is actually useful and that we are in the best position to provide relevancy to our audience." Let's look at a few examples for Lufthansa:

- *Poor idea:* Let's focus on allowing other Lufthansa users to share their thoughts on the best places to travel. This is relevant to Lufthansa's travel base; however, it is a poor idea because there are many companies that already do this better than Lufthansas could hope to develop could as a core competency (Lonely Planet, TripAdvisor, Frommers, etc.). One airline that understood there was already enough good general marketing out in the marketplace attacked this same concept, but from a unique (at least unique at the time) angle. Scandinavian Airlines (SAS) desired to establish close ties with their high-profile, high-income demographic group. They dedicated social media tools to the gay, lesbian, bisexual, and transgender/transsexual community. Gay staff members of SAS provided recommendations and tips on the best venues, night-life, and eateries in Sweden and Denmark. SAS also partnered with several organizations and publishers so the site can offer gay maps, gay guides, and an events calendar that is updated daily. The potential for SAS to be able to market directly to the community of people with the highest propensity to travel is very clear because they found a niche that wasn't being addressed in the general marketplace. Hence, they could truly add value rather than producing a "watered down" version of something already existing. Seems pretty logical, yet company after company misses this important concept—always wanting to build inward-out rather than outward-in.

- *Good idea:* Implement a functionality (wiki) that allows user to see every seat on every plane and allows users to input the pros and cons about each seat. Sites like seatguru.com does this so that is why it is only a good idea, not a great one. But unlike seatguru this makes it easier on the user because it would be specific to Lufthansa's planes, which may configure the same plane differently than other airlines.

- *Great idea:* Why with today's technology do travelers often run into a situation where they run out of the popular meals. For example, the two choices may be beef or chicken and half-way down the aisle the exasperated stewardesses (excuse me, flight attendants) are out of chicken. Why couldn't it work like a wedding when you make your reservation? Or worse, when airlines sell boxed food and you as a flyer are counting on buying one of these delicious (tongue in cheek) boxes on your 5-hour flight, but they run out, and the only thing you have to eat is a pack of gum.

This type of social functionality still will not be 100 percent accurate, but it's much better than the system we have in place today. Also airlines could employ the same concept as trains. Trains have no "speaking" or "cellular phone" sections. Travelers on planes vary by whether they want to talk or whether they want tranquility. The dumb way to do this is to divide the plane into a predetermined number of seats for each flight. This would not work so well. However, if you develop the right social media application, the work would be done by your travelers who wouldn't feel it was work at all, and the process would be fluid and variable from flight to flight.

Love connections could occur on flights more often because more "talkers" would be aggregated and people who don't want to be annoyed by an incessantly boring "talker" need not worry. This could potentially give Lufthansa a competitive advantage in the short term—obviously if this was successful, it would be replicated by the competition. However, the ultimate success, although it might be difficult to replicate would be if through social media you were able to attract a particular crowd (e.g., intelligent, professional, singles, attractive) and that helped define your brand—people would actually choose to fly your airline because of the types of people they would encounter on that airline. Airlines have been fighting to distinguish themselves for years, and this could become a reality. This may be taking things a step too far, but you could have the preppy airline, the grunge airline, middle-class airline, blue collar, and so on.

The executives at Budweiser said that they learned some valuable lessons from their failed YouTube-esque initiative of Bud TV. Let's hope so. They spent $15 million over the first two years alone, and for their efforts, Compete Inc. indicates they don't have enough traffic data to give an accurate reading.[18] They aren't alone though, we are already seeing such popular sites as Dell.com, AT&T.com, Xbox.com, and Apple.com losing site traffic, but they aren't necessarily losing users! Their customers are just spending more time on social media and getting what they need from the companies there. Although it is cliché it's vitally important to fish where the fish are.

The funny thing is that in terms of *Field of Nightmares*, this same flawed replication methodology has repeated itself several times (no pun intended) in this relatively short Internet age. Whether it was e-mail, browsers, portals, search, video, and now social media, many companies believe they will be the starting point rather than an integration point. The example of BellSouth thinking that their users would have a My BellSouth start page (portal) that included weather, sports scores, and stocks is just one example (for the record, people just wanted their phone bill from BellSouth integrated into their established portals, MyYahoo!, iGoogle, etc.) of companies recreating a poorer version of the wheel.

"To help avoid making the same mistakes or our clients making the same mistakes we do a very simple exercise. For the social network example, we have them write down all the features and functionalities they desire on their 'site' or 'social network' onto a transparent piece of acetate. Unbeknownst to them we have all the features and functionality of the technology industry leader (in this case leading social network) on a white piece of paper. We take that acetate and lay it over the white incumbent listing and it is pretty powerful. It usually goes quiet for a few moments, and then we begin discussions on how to appropriate integrate with the leading technology."

Don't build your own Field of Nightmares.

A Truly Interconnected Web?

A key question that remains to be answered (at least at the writing of this book) is about the interconnectivity of the various social media tools. Just like a carmaker doesn't use the same supplier for all of its various parts; rather, they select the best manufacturer for each specialty (e.g., headlights, sun roof, seats). Social media providers can't be the best at every functionality (social network, social bookmarks, wikis, video sharing, photo sharing, etc.). However, users like the simplicity of one-stop shopping and this isn't a new concept. However, corporations do like these walled gardens—these are my toys and nobody else can play! A *walled garden (technology),* with regards to media content, refers to a closed set or exclusive set of information services provided for users (a method of creating a monopoly or securing an information system). This is in contrast to providing consumers access to the open Internet for content and e-commerce.[19] This is primarily due to greed. Some easy to grasp examples of "walled gardens" are

1. AOL's original strategy of containing all of its content exclusively for its Internet subscribers
2. The ability to only get the NFL Game Day Package if you have Direct TV versus regular cable

3. Apple iTunes store—originally having set pricing at $.99 even though the music industry would prefer they have variable pricing (some songs at $.69, others at $1.26) They finally went to this model in 2009 so at least some companies are listening and learning.

"It's a race to see who will work better and faster with everyone else," said Charlene Li, Founder of consulting company Altimeter Group. "It's recognition that you can't be an island of yourself."[20]

Microsoft Outlook tied in contacts, calendar, and e-mail is a good model for how someone will tie up the loose ends of web services.

We've seen this constantly over time, whether it was VHS versus Beta Max, Blue Ray versus High-Definition DVDs, having to fill out the same three forms at the doctor's office with the same information every time you visit a different doctor, and so on. At the time this book was written, there appeared to be two dominant platforms in the social network world: Facebook and Open Social (i.e., MySpace, hi5, iLike, LinkedIn, Google). The hope is that due to the open reliance and nature of social media that this boils down to one, seamless connectivity platform. We have already seen company's willingness to be more open than ever before by Facebook, MySpace, and even Apple allowing programmers access to their systems (via Application Program Interface) to make cool widgets and tools that consumers can enjoy (e.g., Google Maps on the iPhone, Music I like Widgets on MySpace). If this type of cooperation were to occur, it would hyperaccelerate the adoption of social media by the mainstream (Moms and Dads) because there would be more relevant offerings for more people and it would also simplify things. The power user would love it as well because they would have easier access to the best of each type of tool rather than having to wade through various watered down versions (analogous to having all of your clothes, shoes, and glasses from one brand versus getting your sunglasses from Oakley, watch from Rolex, and your jacket from L.L. Bean).

Imagine the ability to only have one login! How nice would that be, along with only a few places to visit when we finally reach an uber-state of truly everything being "pushed" to us rather than us hunting and gathering and putting into one basket—we would have the basket being constantly filled with information goodies from the best and brightest suppliers! With Tools like Facebook Connect and Open ID we are getting close, as these tools allow you to use your existing Facebook IDs to easily access other sites as well as to have your information follow you.

> I have stated all along that I truly feel that in the end game, Facebook and the like will be less of a destination and more of a tool that you use wherever you may happen to be and that it will connect you to other portions of the Web.
> —Natalie Del Conte, CNET TV

You can already see this with the new thinking that has been put forth by Facebook. In particular, the Facebook Connect product is all about openness. The thought behind Facebook Connect and other such platforms is to allow you to take your friends with you, it's what will result in the emergence of the "social web." Instead of trying to hoard all of a user's data, it will be shared on the Discovery Channel site, *San Francisco Chronicle*, Hulu.com, Digg, and so on.

"Everyone is looking for ways to make their websites more social," said Sheryl Sandberg, Facebook's chief operating officer. "They can build their own social capabilities, but what will be more useful for them is building on top of a social system that people are already wedded to."[21]

This type of open thinking is one of the building blocks of the Socialommerce items that we discussed previously. Specifically, this allows people to post a restaurant review on opentable.com and easily share it with their Facebook, MySpace, and so on social graph. Now, if only hospitals and dentists could help me out by only having one form to complete.

Job Recruiting

Another huge shift in the way we do things, both as individuals and as businesses, is the process of job recruitment. To better understand this shift, we should review the established practice of job recruiting and job hunting.

For the past 10 years, if you were attempting to recruit talent, you would pay money to post on job boards like Monster, CareerBuilder, Hot Jobs, and so on. Or you could hire a recruiting firm or headhunter to assist in the recruitment effort. As you will read throughout this book, middlemen are removed in most instances as a result of the social web. In the job recruitment market, middlemen are job boards, job fairs, classified advertisements, and head-hunting firms. For the near future, these traditional recruiting avenues will remain; but their influence will be greatly reduced, and not too far down the line, they will probably vanish altogether. Social networks like Craigslist, LinkedIn, and Plaxo will ultimately take over the recruitment role because they provide more direct and insightful connections between the employer and potential employee.

All of this newfound transparency from social business networks is a godsend for employers. They no longer have to employ a large internal human resource or recruitment staff to perform this type of research, or hire an expensive headhunter. Instead, the potential workforce is already doing this for you (the employer), and they are doing it at much greater depths. Reviewing a résumé in the past was part art and part science; it was necessary to read between the lines on a static piece of paper to formulate whether the person deserved a screening call or interview. Now, social business networks supply photos, videos, links showing a person's actual work, 15 to 20 snapshot references, links to blogs or articles the person may be included in, and so on. If a picture can say a thousand words, then a video résumé must be in the millions, because there is nothing more helpful than this for a recruiter. Recruiters can quickly screen through potential hires in minutes versus all the guesswork associated with traditional paper résumés (paper résumés will still be a nice complement to video résumés).

LinkedIn is a good place to start because they are a quiet but powerful pseudomonopoly. As of the writing of this book, LinkedIn has almost cornered the market on the social business network. This will be tough to supplant because users already have their recommendations on the site. Unless there is an easy way to port these recommendations to a new business network, it would be a somewhat uncomfortable task for people to solicit their previous references to rewrite what had already been posted for a new social business network (this book covers the importance for all social media tools to be interconnected). Imagine having to call your reference and say, "Morning, Carol, this is Ted. I know I haven't spoken to you in three years, but about that nice comment and thumbs-up you gave me on LinkedIn about four years ago, I was wondering if you wouldn't mind signing up for this new job site, after you get your account, which will take six minutes. Can you then write the exact same thing you did for me previously?" That would obviously be no small order. That being said, the hope is that, as previously stated, LinkedIn also figures out how to make the Web more open by allowing your LinkedIn data and recommendations to easily flow and follow you accordingly.

For job seekers, the "always keep your résumé updated" paradigm is gone because now it doesn't even scratch the surface of the importance of maintaining updated information, and more important, updated connections. It is essential to constantly update your career progress on social business networks as well as other social media, web sites, blogs, and so on. It is also much more than simply updating your paper résumés on these sites. It behooves you to have an updated and professional photograph; also, a list of articles that mention you is helpful. A link to your own personal and professional web site with additional information about you will put you a step ahead of the competition. Any radio or video interviews of you should be easily accessible to augment your video résumé. Most important of all is to capture positive feedback and postings from your bosses, peers, partners, and subordinates. In the past, you really only needed one or two solid references from your supervisors.

Previously, once recruiters were able to get potential hires in through the doors, the screening process was difficult at best. It was generally based on a few interviews, a possible call to a reference or two (most likely not), and then your standard background check (this step was also sometimes skipped).

However, that didn't really tell employers the entire story did it? You could be a superstar adored by your boss, but a recruiter may miss the fact that you are a terrible team player, that you treat your peers and subordinates with little respect, and that as a whole, you'd be a detriment to add to an organization that already has good team chemistry. That is why as an individual it is important that you have well-rounded feedback from various divisions and peer groups in and outside the organization. If you skew too heavily one way or another, it may quickly reveal a weakness to your potential employer.

One of the most important things employers look at today is the person's network itself! If the employer is hiring a bunch of new talent and brings on someone who has a polished network, then the new hire instantly becomes a recruiting asset. It was never possible before to have this type of insight into someone's network. You could assume they were connected with people at their current place of work, but you could never confirm it. Bringing on someone who has 300 well-respected professionals in her network is a tremendous asset to any company because after she is hired, the recruited quickly becomes the recruiter.

What really makes networks like LinkedIn helpful is that it allows users to share their online Rolodexes. Shally Steckerl uses social network LinkedIn (industry leader) to more easily recruit talent for Microsoft and other online companies. Steckerl says:

> With my Rolodex, I had to call any one of these thousand people and say, "Hey, Bob. I'm looking for someone that does this, or I'm looking for someone in this industry, or I'm looking for a job, who do you know? With social networking, I don't need to go to Bob directly to find out who Bob's friends are. Or Bob's friends' friends. So, effectively, I have a thousand contacts that could potentially lead me to 100,000, now I have 8,500 contacts that could potentially lead me to 4.5 million.[22]

Echoes Maureen Crawford-Hentz of global lighting company Osram Sylvania, "Social networking technology is absolutely the best thing to happen to recruiting—ever. It's important to load your profile with the right keywords so people like me can find you easily."

It's also important within these social business networks to be constantly building equity. This can be obtained by connecting two people that you have in your network to posting jobs that you are aware of, to giving your peers a thumbs-up and adding written recommendations next to these approval ratings.

Aside from building equity that can be drawn on later, it's imperative that workers proactively manage their "brand" whether they are currently in the job market or not. Employers will perform Google and YouTube searches on a potential recruit's name as well as filter through MySpace, Facebook, and hi5 networks to see what is posted out there. Employers are always looking to mitigate risk. So, even though you may have a 3.9 grade point average and a 1300 SAT score on your résumé, it is immaterial if your hi5 profile picture is of you holding a beer bong while wearing a jockstrap on your head; good luck in landing that dream job!

While I hope you aren't that stupid, you most likely have some friends who are. So it's important to spot-check what is out there and aggressively ferret out potential job career landmines. Job seekers should act like a potential employer and go to the search engines to investigate what shows up when searching for their name. Unflattering items should proactively be removed from the public eye. Part of this search includes confirmation that there aren't any egregious videos out there. Also, if job seekers share a common name with an individual that is less than scrupulous, then the job seeker needs to make certain the employer knows that that person is not them, but rather someone else with the same name. This due diligence and research can take time, so even if you aren't currently in the job market, it's imperative to keep items inside and outside of your business social networks as buttoned up as possible.

Thirteen Virgin Airline employees should have heeded this advice before they were let go from the U.K.-based airline for inappropriate behavior on Facebook. The 13 employees formed a group on Facebook and thought it would be a fun joke to insinuate that there were plenty of cockroaches on the Virgin Airline's planes and that the passengers were generally "chavas." Chava is the British equivalent to calling someone a redneck, or more specifically:

> Chav, Chava or Charva, or Charver or is a derogatory term applied to certain young people in Great Britain. The stereo- typical view of a chava is an aggressive teen or young adult, of working class background, who wears branded sports and casual clothing (baseball caps are also common). Often fights and engages in petty criminality and are often assumed to be unemployed or in a low paid job.[23]

Obviously, the competition among airlines is fierce, so Virgin didn't hesitate to quickly fire these employees for what they deemed insubordination. The world has shifted, and whether we like it our not we are always representing who we are whether we are *on the clock* or not.

Hunters Become the Hunted

The good news for job seekers is that they too also have new and similar powers to check up on a potential employer; thanks in large part to social media. Within these social networks, they have review boards about various employers. And just like in the Kevin Bacon game that uses the famous *Six Degrees of Separation* concept, there is potential that a friend of a friend will have worked for a particular company if a job seeker wants to get the scoop firsthand. Also, along those lines, you can see if anyone in your social business network is interlinked to the person that may ultimately be your boss in the new job. The ability to check on your potential future boss's background along with what other people are saying about that person is very com- forting and useful.

This is also great preparation for the interview, if you know your interviewee is a member of Big Brothers and Big Sisters, you may steer the conversation in that direction. But, even more important, if you are selected for the job, examining the profile of the person who may become your boss will help you decide if you want to work for this person. Do you think you can learn from this new boss; do you have the same theories, aspirations, and approach to work and life?

Other social media tools that are popping up are companies like glassdoor.com. Glassdoor was started by Rich Barton who was also very successful with Expedia and Zillow, both of which opened up information previously not available to end users for travel and real estate. Zillow in particular allowed users to go in and change items listed about their house in wiki format (if there were two bathrooms instead of one, the owner could go in and adjust the data). Glassdoor was started using the concept of "What would happen if someone left the unedited employee survey for the whole company on the printer and it got posted to the Web?"

The site mentions what they do: "Glassdoor.com provides a complete, real-time, inside look at what it's really like to work at a company—ratings, reviews, confidence in senior leadership, and salaries—for free." Well it is free in terms of cash outlay, but the site does require users to share salaries of their current or past positions before they can see salaries that others have posted. The site encourages and demands sharing for the social product to work. Networks like this give the interviewee some power, especially when it comes to salary negotiation because they can see what others in the same position are currently making.

In the past, information on the ins and outs of companies as well as background on potential bosses was limited, if not nonexistent. In a very short time, social media has eliminated this information deficiency. There are even some web-based recruitment companies sprouting up that are looking at a socialommerce model where instead of headhunters getting paid, they actually pay the interviewee money for the opportunity to interview—one such site is called paidinterviews.com. It will be interesting to see if this represents a wave of the future.

A Better Workplace for Employees and Employers

Generally, this makes for a better work environment for employers and employees. It also greatly increases production in companies because the wrong person is less likely to be put into the wrong job. The number of employees leaving within a year will also be reduced because new recruits will have a better sense of what they are getting into (job, boss, company). Also, once employees are in place, now more than ever before, it's essential that they work well with their peers, subordinates, partners, and bosses because their ability to land their next job will depend on it. Skeletons are no longer in the closet; rather, they are in social business networks.

Hiring the Internet Generation

Just as the one-way messaging strategy of advertisers is no longer viable in this new age, it no longer works for employers, either. Millennials or Generation Yers are used to and want collaboration, but they will not necessarily acknowledge or adhere to traditional lines of authority or chains of command. Soon, many baby boomers in executive level positions will retire, and there will be an intense talent fight between companies. Companies can give themselves an advantage by understanding that this new talent has different attitudes, expectations, and skills than the previous generations.

Some people paint members of this under-30 generation as spoiled or lazy. That is far from the truth, they are just different, and in a lot of positive ways. Work and life balance is much more important to them than their parents, and they desire positions that are able to conform to their lifestyle (e.g., work from home or at odd hours). Company beliefs and values need to align with those of employees. A company mission of simply making as much money as possible turns many of this generation off. Companies need to contribute to the greater good of society, to be part of the social community and causes.

Ironically though, if another firm offers Millennials more money or a better opportunity, they will go. There is less loyalty; on average, a person will have 14 different jobs by the time they are 40 years old. Members of this generation have seen that companies in general aren't loyal to their employees, so why should they in turn be loyal to their employers? They desire to stay at the same company and grow, but they understand this probably isn't going to be a reality. They've also seen that companies may only have a strong robust lifespan of 10 to 20 years (e.g., Lycos, Prodigy, Atari, Enron, Circuit City). Fun at work isn't a "nice-to-have"; it is a "need-to-have."

Employers need to throw away the old human resources playbook that consisted of hire, train, manage, and retain. This generation wants collaboration in all aspects of their lives, in part because of the social media tools they grew up with and are accustomed to, but especially because work is where they spend the most time.

Showing up at a college campus for a career fair isn't going to get the job done, because it's a whole new world. Online sites now hold 110 million jobs and 20 million unique résumés. Traditional advertising to attract young talent is as good as burning money. As a company, you need to use everything in your arsenal—blogs, podcasts, social media sites, and so on. However, your current staff members are your best recruiters because they are the ones with the networks and referral power. Just as marketing will be more focused on referral programs, the same holds true for recruiting.

Retaining Talent

By using social media tools during the recruitment process, companies have a better chance of maintaining talent because it's more likely to help put the right person in the right position. However, an employer's work is just beginning when they hire someone. Generation Yers desire constant feedback, and they also evaluate the company from day one. They will not wait around in hopes that things will get better or things will change. There is too much opportunity for them to go to a competitor or even for them to start their own businesses.

Employers are best off exposing new hires to various departments, leaders, and projects. Often the best thing that managers can do is simply "get out of the way" because the young talent may be vastly more talented in certain areas (great hire!). So, instead of traditional management and micromanagement, bosses may be more focused on fostering an environment for success.

Just as employees shouldn't burn bridges, employers shouldn't either. When an employee leaves, it can be bittersweet; but it's important to focus on the "sweet" versus the "bitter" because today, talent may "boomerang" back once they see it's not so great out there. It's imperative that employers not take a smug "we told you so attitude," but rather, take pride in knowing that they must be doing something right if this talent is coming back. Often within social networks, people stay engaged with their previous company through specific groups; that's why Yahoo Alumni and Microsoft Alumni groups on Facebook have 2,300 and 1,600 members respectfully. In a study done in Canada of 18- to 34-year-olds it showed the average person held five full-time jobs by age 27. Rehiring saves money. *Harvard Business Review* indicated it costs roughly half as much to rehire and that person is also 40 percent more efficient in their first 90 days[24]—which intuitively makes sense. Plus, they are also less likely to leave again. The key is for companies to embrace this change in the workforce and to learn as much from Generation Yers as they do from your company.

Southwest Is Not Ding-a-Ling

As we mentioned previously, we have grown accustomed to the news finding us. We have also grown accustomed to other pieces of information finding us rather searching for them. Brands and companies that understand this have benefited and will benefit in the future. Southwest Airlines recognized this early on with its Ding Widget. This widget allows users to place it somewhere convenient (desktop, social network, etc.). For a user who lives in Nashville (Tennessee), whose Mom lives in Birmingham (Alabama), the widget will alert them with a "ding" whenever an appropriate airline ticket sale is available. "After the first year, we hit the 2 million mark for downloads," said a spokesman for Southwest Airlines. It is estimated that the widget receives upwards of 40 million clicks per year. The cost to develop and maintain such a widget is almost at the point of insignificance it is so low.

The key with successful widgets like this is for the companies to show restraint in their push messages. Some smart companies have almost adopted a publisher's model. Historically newspapers and magazines kept their writers in a distinctly different silo than their advertising sales team to ensure that their articles/content were not compromised by pressure from their largest clients. With successful widgets, some companies go to great lengths and in some extreme cases even turn over how these widgets are messaged to the product team versus the marketing team. In the past, many companies have seen with cost-efficient delivery channels (think e-mail) that marketing will spam the user. With these widgets, if you spam the user (in this example, that would be Southwest sending a general reduced-fare message for 20 cities of which neither Nashville nor Birmingham is included) they will be gone.

Speaking of being gone, that is exactly what is happening to some business and personal behaviors. This book highlights that some traditional behaviors, constructs, and principals will continue in this new world, while others will not be suitable. Individuals and businesses face new challenges if they are to stay relevant and viable in this new socialnomic world. Are you up to the challenge?

Chapter Eight Key Points

1. Don't build your own *Field of Nightmares* by building or replicating a social network for your company. If you build it they most likely will not come. You are better off fishing where the fish are and connecting to the best in class social media tools that exist. You aren't a social media company so don't attempt to parade as one.

2. Social media is helping to drive the transformation of mobile devices being the dominant Internet access point than computers.

3. The information exchanged in social media in relation to job searching and recruiting has rendered it unrecognizable from the information exchanged 10 years ago. Appropriate

matches between employer and employee have increased as a result of an increased information flow.

4. The overall achievement of individuals and companies will be largely dependent on their social media success.

5. Just as marketing will become more referral based as a result of rapid information exchanges enabled by social media tools. Job seeking and recruitment will be more referral based than ever before.

6. The younger generations' interpersonal communication skills are starting to suffer as a result of overdependence on nonverbal and non-face-to-face interactions.

7. Search engine results and the traditional Internet advertising model are antiquated—social media will push both of these to revolutionize otherwise they will see a dramatic decrease in market share.

Socialnomics Winners and Losers

Winners

- Good companies and good products.
- Team players (employees).
- Society.
- Democracy.
- Job recruiters.
- Entrepreneurial talent (including musicians, comedians)
- Consumer: Just like in the Barack Obama example, more than ever the American Dream can become a reality. Sure there is still a large advantage to being in the "in" crowd, but more and more you can develop your own crowd using social media's cheap and efficient ability to quickly disseminate ideas and information. As consumers, good products will be easier to find and decisions will be easier to make because recommendations from people you trust and conversations with companies you develop a relationship with will replace the traditional one-way marketing messages.

Losers

- Companies solely reliant on great marketing: all sizzle and no steak is a recipe for failure.
- Undisciplined individuals: individuals exhibiting schizophrenic behavior.
- Companies that DELIBERATE rather than DO will quickly die in a Socialnomic World.
- Middlemen.
- Search engines: assumes the search tools are halfway decent in the social media.
- Traditional advertising agencies.
- Established talent (celebrities, singers, reporters, writers, etc.) that lacks talent.
- Traditional media.

Notes

Introduction

1. James Carville, "It's the economy, stupid." Wikipedia, accessed April 23, 2009, http://en.wikipedia.org/wiki/It%27s_the_economy,_stupid.

2. Barack Obama, Election Night Speech, Chicago, November 4, 2008.

Chapter One

1. Hitwise, June, 2008.

2. Chris Anderson, *The Long Tail* (New York: Hyperion, 2006), Chapter 2.

3. Christoph Marcour, personal interview.

4. Business Analysis and Research, Newspaper Association of America. October 2008, http://www.naa.org/TrendsandNumbers/Advertising-Expenditures.aspx.

5. Daisy Whitney, "SNL Palin Skits: Seen More on Web Than TV," *TVWeek*, October 1, 2008, http://www.tvweek.com/news/2008/10/snl_palin_skits_seen_more_on_w.php.

6. Alan D. Mutter, "$7.5B Sales Plunge Forecast for Newspapers," *Reflections of a Newsosaur,* October 12, 2008, http://newsosaur.blogspot.com/2008/10/75b-sales-plunge-forecast-for.html.

7. Nicholas Carlson, "PC Magazine Goes Out of Print," Silicon Alley Insider, November 19, 2008, http://www.businessinsider.com/2008/11/pc-magazine-goes-out-of-print.

8. [AU: Please provide source info on Playboy magazine statistics.]

9. Alan D. Mutter, "Print Drives Online Ad Sales at Newspapers," *Reflections of a Newsosaur,* February 3, 2009, http://newsosaur.blogspot.com.

10. Jupiter Survey, 2009.

11. Jim Giles, "Internet Encyclopaedias Go Head to Head," *Nature,* December 15, 2005.

12. Brian Morrissey, "Small Brands Teach Big Lessons," *AdWeek*, October 27, 2008, http://www.adweek.com/aw/content_display/news/digital/e3ia353f77f11f28ab959172cf3f7595abb.

13. Mary Schenk, "YouTube Co-Founder Tells Grads to Be Persistent, Take Risks," Department of Computer Science, University of Illinois at Urbana-Champaign, www.cs.uiuc.edu/news/articles.php?id=2007May15-266/.

14. YouTube, April 2009.

15. David Wilson, "American Airlines Crisis Management and Response," *Social Media Optimization,* April 2008, http://social-media-optimization.com/2008/04/american-airlines-crisis-management-and-flyers-response/.

16. Hitwise, 2008.

17. Hitwise, 2008.

Chapter Two

1. C. C. Chapman, "Managing the Gray," May 23, 2008, www.managingthegray.com/2008/05/23/comcast-wins-with-twitter/.

2. "JetBlue Engages in Real Conversation on Twitter," *Socialized,* March 17, 2008, http://www.socializedpr.com/jetblue-engages-in-real-conversation-on-twitter/.

3. Jeff Jarvis, "Dell Hell," *BuzzMachine,* June 21, 2005, http://www.buzzmachine.com/archives/cat_dell.html.

Chapter Three

1. "CMOs Not Ready to Embrace Social Networking Sites, Survey Shows," survey conducted by Epsilon, November 24, 2008, http://www.corporatelogo.com/hotnews/cmo-marketing-social-networking-sites.html.

2. Bill Tily, personal interview

3. Heather Endreas, personal interview.

4. Melissa Dahl, "Youth Vote May Have Been Key in Obama's

Win," msnbc.com, November 5, 2008, http://www.msnbc.msn.com/id/27525497.

5. Facebook Application Statistics.

6. Jerry Seinfeld, http://www.wittcom.com/fear_of_public_speaking.htm.

7. Anick Jesdanun, "OMG! :(It Ain't Write," AP–New York Post, National Commission on Writing at the College Board, April 27, 2008, http://www.nypost.com/seven/04252008/news/nationalnews/omg_it_aint_write_108037.htm?CMP=EMC-email_edition&DATE=04252008

8. "Young Adults Eager to Engage with Brands Online, Global Research from Microsoft and Synovate Reveals," November 11, 2008, http://www.synovate.com/news/article/2008/11/young-adults-eager-to-engage-with-brands-online-global-research-from-microsoft-and-synovate-reveals.html.

9. "Young Adults Eager to Engage with Brands Online, Global Research from Microsoft and Synovate Reveals."

10. "Young Adults Eager to Engage with Brands Online, Global Research from Microsoft and Synovate Reveals."

11. "Advertising Nielsen Online: Kids Encounter Ads Less than Adults," E&P Staff and The Associated Press. October 13, 2008, https://listserv.temple.edu/cgi-bin/wa?A2=ind0810&L=net-gold&D=0&I=-3&T=0&P=58988&F=P.

Chapter Four

1. David Carr and Brian Stelter, "Campaign in a Web 2.0 World," the *New York Times*—Media and Advertising, November 2, 2008, http://www.nytimes.com/2008/11/03/business/media/03media.html?_r=1&ei=5070&emc=eta1.

2. Facebook Fan Data, October 2008.

3. YouTube View Data, October 2008.

4. YouTube View Data, October 2008.

5. Carr and Stelter, "Campaign in a Web 2.0 World."

6. Lance Muller, personal interview, June 2008.

7. Barack Obama, *Barack Obama: Connecting and Empowering*

All Americans Through Technology and Innovation, November 2007, http://www.barackobama.com/pdf/issues/technology/Fact_Sheet_Inno vation_and_Technology.pdf.

8. David Needle, "Huffington: 'Obama Not Elected Without Internet,'" Internetnews.com, November 7, 2008, http://www.internet-news.com/webcontent/article.php/3783741/Huffington+Obama+Not+ Elected+Without+Internet.htm.

9. "Web 2.0 and the Internet Delivered the Vote for Obama," *Huliq News*, November 10, 2008, http://www.huliq.com/2623/72572/web-20-and-internet-delivered-vote.

10. "Web 2.0 and the Internet Delivered the Vote for Obama."

11. Brian Solis, "Is Obama Ready to Be a Two-Way President?," *Tech Crunch*, November 15, 2008, http://www.techcrunch.com/2008 /11/15/is-obama-ready-to-be-a-two-way-president/.

12. Solis, "Is Obama Ready to Be a Two-Way President?"

13. [AU: Please provide source details for note 13 above.]

14. YouTube, October 2008.

15. Burt Helm, "Who's Behind the 'Wassup 2008' Obama Ad? Not Budweiser," *BusinessWeek*—Innovation, October 27, 2008 http://www.businessweek.com/the_thread/brandnewday/archives/200 8/10/whos_behind_the.html.

16. YouTube, October 2008.

17. John McWhorter, *All About the Beat: Why Hip-Hop Can't Save Black America* (New York: Gotham Books, 2008).

18. Ismael AbduSalaam, "Ludacris Explains Controversial Obama Song," *All Hip Hop*, November 6, 2008, http://www.allhiphop.com/ stories/news/archive/2008/11/06/20666656.aspx.

19. Miguel Helft, "Google Uses Searches to Track Flu's Spread," the *New York Times*—Technology, November 11, 2008, http://www.nytimes.com/2008/11/12/technology/internet/12flu.html? 8au&emc=au.

20. Helft, "Google Uses Searches to Track Flu's Spread."

21. Google Trends, April 2008.

22. Google Trends, April 2008.

23. Google Trends, April 2008.

24. Federal News Service, "Campaign Rally with Senator Barack Obama (D IL), Democratic Nominee for President," *Chicago Sun-Times,* October 27, 2008, http://blogs.suntimes.com/sweet/2008/10/obama_closing_argument_speech_1.html.

25. Kate Kay, "Web Ads Mattered More than Ever in 2008 Election," *ClickZ,* November 4, 2008, www.clickz.com/showPage.html?page=clickz_print&id=3631395/.

26. Needle, "Huffington: 'Obama Not Elected without Internet.'"

27. "America Goes to the Polls," *A Report on Voter Turnout in the 2008 Election*, Nonprofit Voter Engagement Network, November 2008, www.nonprofitvote.org/Download-document/America-Goes-to-the-Polls-A-Report-on-Voter-Turnout-in-the-2008-Election.html.

28. Kim Estes, personal interview, November 2008.

29. Facebook Fan Data.

30. "Free Pancakes Anyone?," December 1, 2008, http://social-nomics.net/page/2/.

31. "Free Pancakes Anyone?"

32. Facebook Fan Data.

33. "America Goes to the Polls."

34. "2008 Election Polls: How Long Would You Wait in Line to Vote?" *SodaHead,* November 4, 2008, www.sodahead.com/question/184094/2008-election-polls-how-long-would-you-wait-in-line-to-vote/.35. "Population Division", U.S. Census Bureau, July 1, 2007. http://www.census.gov/popest/states/asrh/SC-EST2007-01.html.

36. Stuart Elliott, "Army to Use Webcasts from Iraq for Recruiting," the *New York Times*, November 11, 2008, http://www.nytimes.com/2008/11/11/business/media/11adco.html?pagewanted=print.

37. Elliott, "Army to Use Webcasts from Iraq for Recruiting."

38. "Army Exceed Recruiting Goal for Fiscal Year 2008," Army.mil/news release, October 10, 2008, http://www.army.mil/-newsreleases/2008/10/10/13228-army-exceed-recruiting-goal-for-fiscal-year-2008/.

Chapter Five

1. "Nielsen Online Global Consumer Survey," Nielsen, April 2007.

2. Stewart Quealy, "Interview: John Gerzema," *SES Magazine*, March 2009, 57.

3. Ken Robbins, Personal Interview.

4. Quealy, "Interview: John Gerzema."

5. iCrossing, "How America Searches: Health and Wellness," January 14, 2008, http://news.icrossing.com/press_releases.php? press_release=icrossing-study-finds-internet-top-resource-for-health-information.

6. "How America Searches."

7. Connie Weatherald, Personal Interview.

8. "How America Searches."

9. YouTube View Data, 2008.

10. ACME Travel, inhouse data.

11. "Jumping the Shark," *Wikipedia*, April 2009, http://en.wikipedia.org/wiki/Jumping_the_shark.

12. Facebook Application Active User Data, April 2008.

13. Razorfish, "The Razorfish Consumer Experience Report 2008," http://feed.razorfish.com/publication/?m=2587&l=1.

14. "The Razorfish Consumer Experience Report 2008."

15. "Credit Union Members Vote on Logo Makeover," *The FinancialBrand.com,* November 21, 2008, http://thefinancialbrand.com /2008/11/21/companion-logo-contest/.

16. "Credit Union Members Vote on Logo Makeover."

17. Quealy, "Interview: John Gerzema."

Chapter Six

1. "Texas Lineman Facebook Status Gets Him Booted Off Team," The World of Issac.com, November 6, 2008, http://www.theworld-ofisaac.com/2008/11/texas-linemans-facebook-status-gets-him.html.

2. "Texas Lineman Facebook Status Gets Him Booted Off Team."

3. B. G. Brooks, "Coaches Deal with Athlete's Social Network," *Rocky Mountain News,* October 12, 2008, www.rockymountain-

news.com/news/2008/oct/12/coaches-deal-athletes-social-networking/.

4. "Patriots Cheerleader Fired After Facebook Swastika Photo," Foxnews.com, November 6, 2008, http://www.foxnews.com/story/0,2933,448044,00.html.

5. Facebook.com, 2008.

6. Tony Blair, "Challenge of Change" (speech, 2008 World Business Forum, New York, September 2008).

Chapter Seven

1. Apple iTunes Podcast Download Data, 2009.

2. "Fantasy Football Today Podcast," ESPN, November 2008.

3. Twitter Postings, October 15, 2008.

4. Twitter Posting, October 21, 2008.

5. "News from the Olympics," Nascar Licensedathletics.com, September 3, 2008, http://nascar.licensedathletics.com/news.php.

6. "Not Ye Old Banners," *The Economist*, November 27, 2008, http://www.economist.com/business/PrinterFriendly.cfm?story_id=12 684861.

7. "Online Ad Spending Grows 10%; Video Ads Strong (Just Not at Google)," *Marketing Pilgrim*, March 31, 2009, http://www.marketingpilgrim.com/2009/03/online-ad-spending-grows-20-video-ads-strong-just-not-at-google.html

8. "March Video Streaming Soars Nearly 40% Compared to Last Year," *Nielsen Wire*, April 13, 2009, http://blog.nielsen.com/nielsenwire/tag/youtube/.

9. Brian Stelter, "Web Site's Formula for Success: TV Content with Fewer Ads," *New York Times,* October 29, 2008, www.nytimes.com/2008/10/29/business/media/29adco.html.

10. [AU: please provide source data for this information.]

11. Stelter, "Website's Formula for Success."

12. Mary Alison Wilshire, personal interview.

13. Stelter, "Website's Formula for Success."

14. Out of Home Advertising Bureau PDF, www.ovab.org/OVAB_ANA_Guide_2008-09.pdf.

15. "Hulu Celebrates First Anniversary, Gains Popularity by Serving Fewer Ads," blog.wired.com, October 29, 2008 http://blog.wired.com/business/2008/10/hulu-turns-one.html.

16. Stelter, "Website's Formula for Success."

17. "OMMA Panel: David vs. Goliath," Online Video Watch, http://www.onlinevideowatch.com/omma-panel-david-vs-goliath/.

18. Facebook Active User Data, 2008.

19. "War of the Words: Scrabulous Is Off Facebook, but Did Hasbro Win the Game?" Knowledge@Wharton, August 6, 2008, http://knowledge.wharton.upenn.edu/article.cfm?articleid=2029.

20. "War of the Words."

21. Facebook 2008.

22. "War of the Words."

23. "War of the Words."

24. Razorfish, "The Razorfish Consumer Experience Report," http://feed.razorfish.com/publication/?m=2587&l=1.

25. Frank Rose, "How Madison Avenue Is Wasting Millions on a Deserted Life," *Wired*, July 24, 2007, www.wired.com/techbiz/media/magazine/15-08/ff_sheep/.

26. Newt Barrett, "Millions for a Virtual Coke on Second Life," *Succeeding Today,* June 25, 2007, http://succeedingtoday.com/2007/07/25/millions-for-a-virtual-coke-on-second-life/.

27. Rose, "How Madison Avenue Is Wasting Millions."

Chapter Eight

1. World Business Forum, Radio City Music Hall, New York, October, 2008.

2. "Student 'Twitters' His Way Out of Egyptian Jail," CNN.com, April 25, 2008, http://edition.cnn.com/2008/TECH/04/25/twitter.buck/.

3. provide information for note

4. Jessica Guynn, "MTV Networks in Deal to Monetize Uploaded Videos," *Los Angeles Times,* November 3, 2008, www.latimes.com/business/la-fi-myspace3-2008nov03,0,6256914.story.

5. Steve O'Hear, "MTV and MySpace Partner to monetize pirated content," ZDNET, November 3, 2008, http://blogs.zdnet.com/

social/?p=602.

6. Organizing for America, http://www.barackobama.com/issues/technology/.

7. Author's estimate.

8. Erik Schonfeld, "Google Makes Up 88 Percent of Mozilla's Revenues, Threatens Its Non-Profit Status," TechCrunch, http://www.techcrunch.com/2008/11/19/google-makes-up-88-percent-of-mozillas-revenues-threatens-its-non-profit-status/.

9. 2008 Interactive Advertising Bureau Online Marketing Report.

10. Pubmatic AdPrice Index Q4 2008, http://www.pubmatic.com/adpriceindex/AdPriceIndex_Quarterly_Q4_08.pdf.

11. Patrick Smith, "Digital Media: Facebook, Yahoo, Microsoft Profit From Open Networks In Europe," March 9, 2009, http://www.paidcontent.co.uk/entry/419-ft-digital-media-facebook-yahoo-microsoft-profit-from-open-networks-in-/.

12. "College Student and Teen Web Tastes," *eMarketer*, November 19, 2008, www.emarketer.com/Article.aspx?id=1006736/.

13. Todd Young, personal interview.

14. "Is the Mobile Web Replacing the Wired Web in Southeast Asia?," Fierce Wireless, November 20, 2008, http://www.fiercewireless.com/press-releases/mobile-web-replacing-wired-web-southeast-asia.

15. Sidhaarthaa Bezboraa, "Mobile Social Networking Use Grows 182% over 2007 in US, March 17, 2009," http://www.wireless-duniya.com/?p=1062.

16. Mark Walsh, "Buzzwire Unveils Mobile Social Site," MediaPostNews, http://www.mediapost.com/publications/?fa=Articles.showArticle&art_aid=100709.

17. https://generationfly.com/lounge.

18. [AU: please provide information for note.]

19. *Wikipedia,* s.v. "walled garden (technology)," http://en.wikipedia.org/wiki/Walled_garden_(technology) (accessed December 21, 2008.

20. Microsoft's New Windows Live Aims to Be Hub for Web, InfoTech.TMCnet.com, November 13, 2008, http://it.tmcnet.com/

news/2008/11/13/3783709.htm.

21. "Facebook Aims to Extend Its Reach Across the Web," SM2, http://www.sm2.com.au/content/view/777/76/.

22. NPR Radio, *Weekend Edition Saturday,* November 22, http://www.npr.org/templates/archives/rundown_archive_hub.php?date=11-22-20082006.

23. *Wikipedia,* s.v. "chava," http://en.wikipedia.org/wiki/Chav (accessed 11/25/2008.

24. *Harvard Business Review.*

About the Author

Over his 15-year career, Erik Qualman has helped grow the online marketing and e-business functions of Cadillac, AT&T, Yahoo, EarthLink, Travelzoo, and EF Education.

Qualman is a frequently requested speaker within the Internet and marketing communities. He has been highlighted in numerous publications including *BusinessWeek*, *AdvertisingAge*, *Forbes*, *Investor's Business Daily*, *eWeek*, *Media Life*, *Adweek*, *TechCrunch*, *Direct Marketing News*, *Marketing FM*, and *Direct Response Magazine*. He has also been interviewed on various radio, television, and Internet outlets. Qualman has previously authored works of fiction, including the political thriller *Crisis*.

As of 2009, Qualman is the Global Vice President of Online Marketing for EF Education, headquartered in Lucerne, Switzerland. EF Education is the world's largest private educator. Qualman works out of EF's 850-person Cambridge, Massachusetts, office.

Qualman holds a BA from Michigan State University and an MBA from the University of Texas at Austin. He was first team Academic All-Big 10 for basketball at Michigan State.

Qualman is a paid columnist for Search Engine Watch and contributing writer to *SES Magazine*. He also maintains the social media blog socialnomics.net. In his spare time he enjoys SCUBA diving, golfing, tennis, and MSU hoops, and he has been fortunate to travel to 37 countries. He lives with his wife, Ana Maria, in Boston.

He is also founder of the charitable organization Paperback Robin Hood.